DEVIL'S ADVOCATES

DEVIL'S ADVOCATES is a series of books devoted to exploring the classics of horror cinema. Contributors to the series come from the fields of teaching, academia, journalism and fiction, but all have one thing in common: a passion for the horror film and a desire to share it with the widest possible audience.

'The admirable Devil's Advocates series is not only essential - and fun - reading for the serious horror fan but should be set texts on any genre course.'
Dr Ian Hunter, Reader in Film Studies, De Montfort University, Leicester

'Auteur Publishing's new Devil's Advocates critiques on individual titles... offer bracingly fresh perspectives from passionate writers. The series will perfectly complement the BFI archive volumes.' **Christopher Fowler,** *Independent on Sunday*

'Devil's Advocates has proven itself more than capable of producing impassioned, intelligent analyses of genre cinema... quickly becoming the go-to guys for intelligent, easily digestible film criticism.' *Horror Talk.com*

'Auteur Publishing continue the good work of giving serious critical attention to significant horror films.' *Black Static*

 DevilsAdvocatesbooks

 DevilsAdBooks

T0312991

DEVIL'S ADVOCATES

HALLOWEEN

MURRAY LEEDER

Acknowledgments

There are many people to thank. First and foremost among them is John Atkinson for giving me the vote of confidence to take on the project of writing about one of my favourite horror films, and providing a firm editorial hand. I need also need to thank Rhett Miller, Ben Wright, Dan Sheridan and Drew Beard for their varied contributions, as well as my loving wife Alana Conway. Finally, infinite thanks to John Carpenter for consenting to several stimulating conversations; they say you shouldn't meet your idols, but it's nice to see it works out some of the time.

First published in 2014 by
Auteur, 24 Hartwell Crescent, Leighton Buzzard LU7 1NP
www.auteur.co.uk
Copyright © Auteur 2014

Series design: Nikki Hamlett at Cassels Design
Set by Cassels Design www.casselsdesign.co.uk
Printed and bound by CPI Group (UK) Ltd, Croydon, CR0 4YY

British Library Cataloguing-in-Publication Data
A catalogue record for this book is available from the British Library

ISBN: 978-1-906733-79-7 (paper)
ISBN: 978-1-906733-86-5 (e-book)

CONTENTS

INTRODUCTION

SYNOPSIS

Into a pumpkin's eye.

Halloween's title sequence features a glowing jack o' lantern framed by blackness, starting in the left of the screen but getting closer and closer until its left eye fills the frame. Following this, *Halloween*'s action starts on October 31, 1963 in Haddonfield, Illinois, in a long, unbroken subjective camera shot. From the perspective of an unknown character, we watch unseen as a teenage girl makes out with her boyfriend on the family couch. As they withdraw to an upstairs bedroom, the figure enters the house, withdraws a butcher knife, dons a mask lying on the floor (a masking effect over the camera) and then stabs the girl to death. Leaving the house, the figure is unmasked and we get the first reverse shot in the film to see a six-year-old boy dressed a clown, silent and holding a bloody knife before his bewildered parents. The child murderer is Michael Myers (Will Sandin as child, Tony Moran as adult, Nick Castle as 'The Shape'), and the victim was his 15-year-old sister Judith (Sandy Johnson).

On October 30, 1978, Michael's psychiatrist, Dr. Sam Loomis (Donald Pleasence), arrives to collect him from an asylum at Smith's Grove, Illinois, for a court appearance. Michael has spent the last fifteen years catatonic, silent and unresponsive. When Loomis and Nurse Chambers (Nancy Stephens) arrive, there has been a prisoner escape. While Loomis is investigating, Michael attacks Chambers, steals the car and drives away.

Our first look at Michael Myers, unmasked as a six-year-old murderer.

The morning after, in Michael's hometown of Haddonfield, we meet Laurie Strode (Jamie Lee Curtis), a bookish teenager. On behalf of her realtor father, she delivers keys to the Myers house where the murder of Judith took place; Michael observes from the inside, and follows her outside to watch her walk away, breathing heavily. Laurie and her more outgoing and sexually-experienced friends Annie Brackett (Nancy Loomis) and Lynda Van Der Klok (P.J. Soles) go about their day unaware of the fact that Michael is stalking them. Laurie catches glimpses of Michael, now wearing a mysterious white mask and a work uniform stolen from a murdered tow-truck driver, but dismisses them as delusions.

An over-the-shoulder shot of Michael watching Laurie.

Meanwhile, Dr. Loomis arrives in Haddonfield. Though the local police, including Annie's father, Sheriff Brackett (Charles Cyphers), are sceptical, Loomis is convinced that Michael will return home and relive the crime he committed as a child. He believes that Michael is pure evil, lacks any human emotions, and will certainly kill again. Loomis also discovers that Judith Myers' headstone has been stolen from the cemetery.

Laurie is spending the evening babysitting for young Tommy Doyle (Brian Andrews), as well as Lindsey Wallace (Kyle Richards), whom Annie is meant to be babysitting but whom Annie dumps on Laurie in order to meet her boyfriend. Tommy sees Michael and is convinced he is 'the boogeyman', but Laurie dismisses his concerns. But Michael kills Annie, strangling her in her car, and then Lynda and her boyfriend Bob (John Michael Graham), murdering them after furtive sex.

Unable to contact her friends, Laurie leaves the children and goes to investigate. She finds Annie's body lying on a bed with the tombstone of Judith Myers sitting above her, and also Bob and Lynda's bodies displayed ritualistically around the room. Michael attacks her with a butcher knife but she escapes, returning to the Doyle house and stabbing Michael in the neck with the knitting needle. Finding the children in the upper room, she tells them that she's killed him, but Tommy replies, 'You can't kill the boogeyman'. Indeed, Michael reappears, and Laurie lets the children run from the house before taking refuge in an upstairs closet.

Laurie discovers this gruesome display.

As Loomis sees the children fleeing the house, Laurie twists a coat hanger into a weapon as Michael tries to break into the closet. She pokes him in an eye, he drops his knife and she stabs him with it. He collapses but comes back a third time and tries to strangle Laurie. Loomis arrives but cannot take a clear shot. Struggling, Laurie pulls off Michael's mask and after he takes the time to put it back, Loomis shoots him repeatedly. Michael falls from a balcony. Through her cries, Laurie says, 'It was the boogeyman'.

'As a matter of fact, it was,' says Loomis, and walks over to the balcony. Michael's body is gone. Loomis's face reflects not surprise, but confirmation. The film ends with a montage of the places where Michael has been throughout the film, ending with the Myers' place, a Strode Realty 'For Sale' sign visible in front of it. Michael's heavy breathing is heard over top of the montage, but we do not see him again.

A STYLISTIC EXERCISE?

For anyone who's never seen *Halloween*, the above summary may not suggest a cinematic classic. It may actually sound more hackneyed and cliché-ridden. In terms of the broad outlines of the plot, the film can make no great claims for originality. As writer-director John Carpenter states on the commentary track for *Halloween* originally recorded for the 1994 Criterion Laserdisc, 'Perhaps all the sequences in *Halloween* are familiar to the audience. They've seen them before in horror movies. They're simply being restated; kind of classic horror setups, reworked slightly'. His words correspond with what Philip Brophy would write a few years after *Halloween* came out:

> The contemporary horror film *knows* that you've seen it before; it *knows* that you know what is about to happen; and it knows that you know it knows you know. And none of it means a thing, as the cheapest trick in the book will still tense your muscles, quicken your heart and jangle your nerves. (2000: 279, original emphasis)

Halloween knows all this, certainly, and is unashamed to go for the cheapest trick in the book ... and to remind us why the trick worked to begin with. *Halloween*'s self-consciousness about its place in its genre is signalled by gestures towards the history of horror. It makes numerous references, for instance, to *Psycho* (1960), clearly exalting Hitchcock's masterpiece as an ur-text from which it is borrowing, and perhaps even positioning itself as *Psycho*'s spiritual sequel. It is also one of the earliest horror films to depict characters *watching* horror films.[1] In this case, the children (and, briefly, Laurie), watch *The Thing from Another World* (1951) and *Forbidden Planet* (1956), showing as part of a Halloween marathon hosted by 'Doctor Dementia', presumably one of the TV horror hosts who were such a key part of the rediscovery of Golden Age horror by the children of the 1950s (Skal, 2001: esp. 237-41, 265-8). It is knowing and self-reflexive about its place within its genre, but in a way that avoids the extravagant metafictional conceits of such later films as *Fright Night* (1985), *Scream* (1996) and *The Cabin in the Woods* (2012).

A large part of the effectiveness of *Halloween* lies in its willingness to be basic and uncomplicated. Even its stylistic flourishes, highly ambitious for such a low-budget independent production, are smoothly integrated, instead of being showy and ostentatious. *Halloween* is inseparable from the Panaglide/Steadicam shots that make the film feel mobile and floating (and which makes its stillnesses all the more meaningful by contrast), the Anamorphic widescreen compositions of which Carpenter makes such careful use, and of course the musical score by Carpenter himself. Synthesizer music ages a film like nothing else (perhaps the most dated element of *Apocalypse Now* [1979] is Carmine Coppola's tinny score), but *Halloween* is unimaginable without its score, both the iconic theme and the more atmospheric incidental music that works wonders in keeping the tension alive through the film's slower patches.

Carpenter has characterised *Halloween* as an exercise in style (Boulenger, 2001: 97), and freely uses the term 'exploitation film' to describe it (author interview). He is not being disparaging, as he tends to discuss *Halloween* with affection and pride. *Halloween* has plenty to offer besides style, but its sense of style is surely the reason for its lasting effectiveness. To be sure, *Halloween* does have its share of technical flaws and it shows its low budget seams in places, but the film's straightforwardness helps ensure that these only become evident on repeat viewings. Pasadena substitutes unconvincingly for rural Illinois; palm trees are even visible in the distance. The foliage of even the more regionally appropriate trees is awfully lush and green for late October, and yet there are periodically dead leaves on the ground.[2] Yet somehow, almost mysteriously, the film still *feels* like Halloween. It captures the spirit that Ray Bradbury wrote of a few years earlier in his young adult book *The Halloween Tree*: 'Anyone could see that the wind was a special wind this night, and the darkness took on a special feel because it was All Hallows' Eve' (1972: 4). The wide, bare streets resonate with menace even in the film's mundane moments, and every pumpkin's smile seems as threatening as it is friendly.

Halloween is an acknowledged horror classic, and one of the relatively few horror films added to the National Film Registry by the U.S. Library of Congress, an honour accorded to it in 2006. And yet there is more to *Halloween* (the franchise and phenomenon) than *Halloween* (the film). There have been seven sequels (only the first two of which had any involvement by Carpenter), a remake with its own sequel (and, at this writing, another purportedly in production), plus novelizations, young adult novel spinoffs, comic books, video games and merchandise of all sorts, not to mention a slate of making-of documentaries. *Halloween* is a franchise, and a lucrative one. Even outside of the official confines of the franchise, there are fan forums online, fan films galore on YouTube, and 2011 even saw duelling pornographic parodies, *Halloween XXX Porn Parody* (by Smash Pictures) and *Official Halloween Parody* (by Zero Tolerance), in which the sexual subtext of the original film gets pushed to absurd extremes. Yet this book is not about *Halloween* the franchise or *Halloween* the phenomenon, but about the first film on its own. It will not be taken for granted, for instance, that Laurie Strode is Michael Myers' long-lost sister, a twist introduced in *Halloween II* (1981) and taken as gospel in Rob Zombie's remake (2007). Though this revelation does indeed come from the typewriter of John Carpenter, who scripted the sequel, Carpenter confesses that it was a last minute invention that was not conceived during the making of the first film. He tells me:

> That was purely a function of having decided to become involved in the sequel to this movie where I didn't think there was really much of a story left. What was I going to say? There was nothing more to say. That night's done, that story's over. Why are we beating this to death? But I couldn't stop it from being made. So I went ahead and decided to write the script … whoa, I didn't do a very good job, but that was one of the things that came out. The second script … mainly, dealt with a lot a beer sitting in front of a typewriter saying 'what the fuck am I doing? I don't know.' (author interview)

He added that the idea of Laurie being Michael's sister 'makes no sense. It's just silly.

Foolish'. The twist does little to enhance *Halloween*, clarifying Michael Myers' motivations when the film is most effective when they remain vague, and also literalising a dynamic between Michael and Laurie that is muted in the first film.[3] This book, then, will not take it as gospel. Much less will this book assume that Michael Myers' is being controlled by a group of evil neo-druids called the Cult of Thorn, as 'revealed' in *Halloween: The Curse of Michael Myers* (1995), the film generally thought of as the series' nadir. Who can honestly be expected to watch *Halloween* and see the sanatorium director, Dr. Wynn (Robert Phelan), a character who appears in one scene, as the secret villain behind everything?

In a way, it seems hard to begrudge writers wanting to 'explain' Michael Myers. One might quibble with such explanations as a long-lost sister, an evil druidic conspiracy or even an ancient Irish curse (as in the novelisation we will discuss later), but a long-running series built around a shadowy, inexplicable, unmotivated foe, may be a tougher sell. Yet for a single film of 90 minutes, especially one as atmospheric and effective as *Halloween*, it works so much better than it would have with some tacked-on, hackneyed explanation. In the documentary *Halloween: A Cut Above the Rest*, Carpenter speaks about resisting the temptation to conjure up some hokey curse to explain Michael and his powers . . . a temptation that got the better of several others of Michael's interpreters.

HALLOWEEN AND THE SLASHER FILM

Halloween is inseparable in the minds of many from the slasher film.[4] In the BBC series *A History of Horror* (2010), presenter Mark Gatiss describes *Halloween* as 'the consummate slasher movie', but adds, 'I'm not so enthusiastic about its legacy. A slough of lower-quality, increasingly gory serial killer outings that would overwhelm the genre for years to come, like horror's equivalent of Dutch Elm Disease'. This strategy of condemning the slasher film all the better to praise *Halloween* (and vice versa) is not new. In a 1980 episode of their PBS show *Sneak Previews*, Roger Ebert and Gene Siskel devoted an episode to condemning the violent new crop of horror films but held *Halloween* (which they both reviewed positively two years earlier) up as an exception. After showing the closet sequence from near the end of *Halloween*, Ebert stated:

One of the things a short scene can't show you is that *Halloween* is directed and acted with a great deal more artistry and craftsmanship than the sleazebucket movies we've been talking about. But there's another, much more important difference. As you watch *Halloween* your basic sympathies are always enlisted on the side of the woman, not with the killer. The movie develops its women characters as independent, intelligent, spunky and interesting people. *Halloween* does not hate women.

Then Siskel shifted the issue back to craftsmanship: 'Not only does *Halloween* not hate women, but it loves film,' and he praised the striking composition of the sequence, including the blue horizontal lines projected through the slats of the closet door. Ebert agreed that, 'artistry can redeem any subject matter'. This seems to me to be a nebulous defence of *Halloween* (summed up by John McCarthy as 'it is artistically valid to hack up independent female characters on screen, as long as you do it with suspense and flair' [(1984: 150)]), but it tells us something about the legitimacy that has historically been bestowed on the film: the exalted example of the slasher film that serves to damn all the rest.

To say the least, *Halloween*'s relationship to the slasher film is a complex one. The label can only be used on the film retrospectively. As Mark Jancovich writes:

> Carpenter had little or no sense of making a slasher movie and many critics at the time saw [*Halloween*] as a startlingly clever, knowing and self-conscious play with the genre. Carpenter could not have seen *Halloween* as a slasher movie because there was no such category at the time. (2002: 8)

The most perceptive account of the relationship of *Halloween* to the slasher film comes from Richard Nowell in *Blood Money: A History of the First Teen Slasher Film Cycle* (2011). Nowell delineates a set of stages for a film cycle beginning with a Pioneer Production, followed by a Speculator Production (potentially a Trailblazer Hit), which is in turn followed by various Prospector Cash-ins, Reinforcer Hits and finally Carpetbagger Cash-ins. *Halloween* falls into the category of Speculator Production, which builds tentatively on the conventions laid out in a Pioneer Production, as well as the definitive Trailblazer Hit. The Pioneer Production, the film that triggered the slasher film cycle well before it had a name or identity, was the Canadian horror film *Black Christmas* (1974), directed by Bob Clark. The Prospector Cash-ins immediately following *Halloween*, borrowing as much as possible from it in hopes of inheriting some of its success, yielded a few Reinforcer Hits, notably *Friday the 13th* (1980) and *Prom Night* (1980) (Nowell, 2011: 41–56). As many scholars have discussed, this body of films often appeals to both a prurient and juvenile obsession with sexuality and a conservative attitude towards it. As Michael Ryan and Douglas Kellner say, 'There is a contradiction between the explicitly erotic scenes and the puritanical message of many of the movies. Perhaps they are simply symptoms of a culture which is fascinated with sex but which still thinks of it in terms of guilt and transgression' (1998: 191).

A great part of what the slasher films that followed took from *Halloween* was aesthetic. Many of them borrowed extensively from *Halloween*'s minimalist score, its blue-tinged night-time cinematography, and its roving, subjective camera work. The latter would be much criticised, the aesthetic choice to allow the audience to see through the eyes of the killer accused of delivering disguised rape fantasy.[5] The bulk of these films have whodunit elements, in contrast to *Halloween* where, beyond the opening sequence, the identity of the killer is never in doubt. In many later slashers (perhaps first *Friday the 13th*), the point-of-view shots serve to preserve a narrative surprise by concealing the identity of the killer, but where they have a more expressive or stylistic purpose in *Halloween*, which lacks whodunit elements. But perhaps *Halloween*'s most important point of influence on the slasher films to follow was through the Laurie Strode character, the 'Final Girl'. This term was coined by Carol J. Clover in her influential 1987 article 'Her Body, Himself: Gender in the Slasher Film', later expanded into the 1992 book *Men, Women and Chain Saws: Gender in the Modern Horror Film*, from which I cite here:

> She is the one who encounters the mutilated bodies of her friends and perceives the full extent of the preceding horror and of her own peril; who is chased, cornered, wounded; who we see scream, stagger, fall, rise, and scream again. She is abject terror personified. (1992: 35)

But what's more, she is the one who is allowed to take up a weapon and defeat the villain herself – more fully in later slasher films than is the case in *Halloween*. She is paradoxically both disempowered and empowered.[6] She is smart, resourceful and observant, and in one of the most criticized aspects of the slasher film, often virginal and repressed or at least more conservative in behaviour than the 'disposable', sexualised women around her. Clover resists reading the Final Girl as legitimately feminine, but rather sees her as a figure of transvestism, a boy in drag: 'to the extent that she means "girl" at all, it is only for purposes of signifying male lack ... To applaud the Final Girl as a feminist development ... is, in light of her figurative meaning, a particularly grotesque expression of wishful thinking' (1992: 53).[7]

While the Final Girl has important predecessors in *Psycho*, *The Texas Chain Saw Massacre* (1974) and perhaps even *Nosferatu* (1922), Laurie codified the character archetype that would be repeated many times. Some later Final Girls are arguably more progressive feminist figures than Laurie herself; Kyle Christensen argues that Laurie is an antifeminist Final Girl, reflective of a male 'Cult of True Womanhood' (2001: 27–9), and that Nancy Thompson of *A Nightmare on Elm Street* (1984) is a better representation of the Final Girl's feminist potential. In fact, in her own study of the slasher film, Vera Dika argues for Laurie as just such a 'traditional female' in the patriarchal vein: 'She incorporates a man's set of values, applies them to tradition women's roles, and is sexually passive' (1990: 47), as opposed to her friends, whom she identifies as grotesque parodies of feminist types. While Laurie is surely a patriarchal woman (she spends much of the film wearing an apron and her makeshift weapons, a knitting needle and a coat hanger, have obvious domestic implications), I find it hard to follow this argument to the extreme that Dika does: Annie and Lynda are certainly ultimately 'disposable' in narrative terms, but, perhaps because Debra Hill wrote much of their dialogue, they are given plenty of characterisation and likeable quirks. They are made into individuals, rather than simple fodder, and while the audience is not precisely given to mourn their deaths as tragedies, neither are their deaths seen as necessary or as causes for celebration (compare, say, the death of Paris Hilton's character in *House of Wax* [2005], which one looks forward to from the moment she appears on the screen). One feminist scholar admires the way that 'Laurie's characterization obviously extols self-realisation above conformity, displaying a maturity ... that refutes any simplistic equation between sexual "liberation" and independence' (Short, 2006: 46). There is, of course, a distinction to be made between saying that Michael wants to punish promiscuous teens and that Carpenter does (Carpenter tells me that he saw Laurie as the anomalous one and the other girls as behaving appropriately: 'I don't want to kill promiscuous girls! I love promiscuous girls!').[8] And the question looms: if Michael is out to punish sexually active girls, why does he want to kill Laurie at all?

None of this is to absolve *Halloween* of sexism, precisely, and though I do not suspect Carpenter and his collaborators of conscious misogyny, I have never been fully convinced by his counter-explanations, either. In a 1981 interview, Todd McCarthy suggested that Annie and Lynda are punished for their sexual activity and Carpenter retorts: 'No, they're unaware because they're involved in something else. They're interested in their boyfriends, so they're ignoring the signs' (1981: 24). Yet surely there are lots of ways to represent a character as distracted that do not involve sex. Interestingly, Carpenter also insists in that interview that it is not virginity per se but unleashed sexual repression that frees and empowers Laurie, a point to which I will return.

For the moment, let us be content to acknowledge that *Halloween* is clearly related to the slasher cycle, but is an entity distinct from it. In many respects, one is actually struck today by how *unlike* the slasher film *Halloween* is. One of the most obvious is pacing; *Halloween*'s slow, deliberate setup and drawn-out suspense sequences may actually remind viewers more of the 'quality horror films' of the 1950s and '60s (like *The Innocents* [1961], an acknowledged influence on Carpenter) than the quick-cut, impatiently paced and blood-soaked slasher films that would follow. The body count of four (five if you count the barely-glimpsed body of the tow truck driver whom Michael kills off screen) is negligible by the slaughterhouse standards of 1980s slasher films, and *Halloween* is next to bloodless, with the only fake blood in the film appearing in the opening sequence and in the superficial cut to Laurie's arm. And *Halloween* is wonderfully atmospheric, something one can say of few slasher films; at its best (say, the composition of Michael silhouetted against the white background of the Wallace house, as spied by Tommy Doyle), one would venture to call it elegant, even beautiful. The project of this book is not precisely to rescue *Halloween* from the slasher film (it does not need rescuing), but to understand and appreciate it on other terms. Some writers (notably Driscoll [2011]) have even taken to calling the film *Halloween 1*, perhaps in an analogue to using the name *Star Wars: Episode IV: A New Hope* in place of its original title, *Star Wars* (1977).[9] However, this has the unfortunate effect of resituating *Halloween* in relation to its sequels. While it would be foolish to pretend the series does not exist, *Halloween*'s sequels have done the original few favours, except for illustrating its greatness by contrast. Carpenter tells me that he has watched many but not all of them. He also says that, if he had his way, there would not have been any film but the first one.

Michael silhouetted against the Wallace house.

WHAT DOES MICHAEL MYERS WANT?

Before interviewing Carpenter for the first time in August 2012, I asked the students in my class on horror films what they thought I should ask him about. The bulk of them suggested that I ask what motivates Michael Myers, and in particular, the murder of his sister Judith. I half-expected the answer Carpenter ultimately gave: 'Beats me!' When asked why he thinks people want an answer at all, he told me, 'I don't know, I don't know, 'cause it's maybe dramatically not satisfying'. Where one *Halloween* can get by on ambiguity, the franchise, it was assumed, demands defined motivations for its villain.

As I have noted, *Halloween* lacks whodunit elements, but does that make it a whydunit? The novelisation gives one explanation for why Michael kills; the later films give a range of different (and increasingly bizarre) explanations. His mysterious motivations lend themselves to so many interpretations that they give rise to priceless exchanges like this one, from an interview with Carpenter by R.A. the Rugged Man:

R.A.: Is Michael Myers a virgin?

J.C.: Is he a virgin?

R.A.: I mean, all he does is kill. Did he ever get laid?

J.C.: I don't think he was able to. He was fucked up, I think he got confused between fucking and killing.

R.A.: What if he's really just a repressed homosexual on a rampage?

J.C.: I never thought about that. I just think he's crazy. But what do I know, maybe he is. (2001)

The best question may not be 'why does Michael kill Judith?' so much as 'why does he appear to have killed her?' Was it punishment for her underage sexuality (Michael acting as a moral guardian)? Or was it an expression of his own sexual desire, an Oedipal act displaced onto the kitchen knife because his youth precluded actual sexual activity? Or some combination of both? Or something else entirely? Some scholars have argued against the notion that it is simple punishment for her sexual activity: as William Paul writes, 'Reading sexual desire into this without accounting for the age of the child seems to me only slightly less perverse than the sequence itself' (1994: 485). Reynold Humphries suggests that, building on the film's pervasive theme of repression, we can say that:

Michael has no idea of *why* he kills his sister … Unconsciously, Michael is killing, not his sister, but his mother for choosing someone else. Surely it is of the greatest importance that Michael should put on a mask, hardly a way of hiding his identity; his sister must recognize him. The mask then symbolizes Michael's refusal to be looked at, to become the object of the other's look, to recognize the other as having the same rights and desires as himself. Michael has not passed beyond the mirror stage and cannot let anyone into his world as this would be to destroy himself as narcissistic centre of the world and his relation with his mother as the sole relationship that matters. (2002: 140)

Supporting Humphries' explanation is the fact that Judith, as a babysitter, is literally acting *in loco parentis*. And yet surely this reading would be more convincing if the film did anything to establish Michael's mother as a character, or even as a figure of thematic importance; she is seen only fleetingly and never mentioned again. Even the single word of dialogue attributed to her in the screenplay ('Michael?') is given to the father instead in the finished film.

Mikel J. Koven suggests another, related possibility, that Michael's motivation is punishing neglectful babysitters: 'Michael's original attack on his sister, Judith, was not so much about her having sex as it was about her not being responsible for babysitting her younger brother. Sex is merely an extension of neglect as a result of poor babysitting' (2008: 124). This approach raises questions of its own (again: why then would Michael want to kill Laurie, since she's an obvious candidate for babysitter-of-the-century?). Nonetheless, Koven's interpretation has the value of recognising babysitting as being at the core of *Halloween*.

This lack of consensus as to Michael's motivations leads us to a point that may seem obvious and banal: he does not exactly have one, or at least not one that we can know. 'Profiling' Michael is a fool's errand. This is not to say that any of the scholars described above have been wasting their time; I think all of their investigations have been helpful and insightful, but finally none of their answers are fully satisfying. Hopefully, saying that Michael Myers does not have a motivation is not avoiding the issue, but confronting a reality of the film. Michael Myers is not constructed an as individual instance of human pathology – this despite the film's overlay of psychoanalysis, which I will discuss later. He is something more abstract. He is a ghost, or one of the implacable murderers from urban legends, or even, as I shall argue later, an inexplicable threat analogous to one of H. P. Lovecraft's cosmic monsters.

URBAN LEGENDS AND LEGEND TRIPPING

Vera Dika notes that: 'In its designation of place, *Halloween* has introduced a tendency toward a paradigmatic, almost mythical representation. This tendency is continued in its representation of time' (1990: 35). This is one of the reasons why it has aged so well. Despite obvious markers of the 1970s in terms of costume and cinematic technique, the film resists the temptation to put hip, slangy dialogue in its characters' mouths or to establish many specifics about Haddonfield beyond its status as a middle-American everytown. Very little separates the film's 1963 from 1978, in part because the film does not really take place at any specific time or place, but rather within its own mythical space, one strongly affiliated with the space of the American urban legend. Less than a year after *Halloween* was released, a review in the journal *Western Folklore* by Larry Danielson noted the film's extensive affiliations with this perverse brand of American mythology. Danielson calls it 'a colourful mosaic of urban legend themes and motifs' (1979: 214), including an escaped lunatic on the loose, a killer attacking from a car roof, a frightened woman taking refuge in a closet, mysterious phone calls replete with heavy breathing, a killer hiding in the back seat of a car, a killer who vanishes without a trace, and of course a local house that has taken on the status of legend due to something terrible that happened there once. Writes Danielson:

> All of these motifs are found in varying configurations in common urban legends, in for example, stories about the assaulted babysitter, the roommate's death, the hook-man, and the assailant in the back seat. In *Halloween* these elements are melded together to create a film text that provides the audience with physiological and emotional responses often encountered in the urban legend narration. (1979: 218)

He further notes that the film's themes of feminine weakness and the dangers of promiscuous sexuality are quite congruent with many modern American urban legends as well.

The urban legend elements of *Halloween* have also been noted by Koven, who particularly cites the film's links to a legend called 'The Babysitter and the Man Upstairs' (2008: 123), which is also the source of *When a Stranger Calls* (1979).[10] I shall discuss this legend later in the book. Also, Carpenter has said that urban legends of deranged killers on the loose helped him conceive the plot for *Halloween*, as well as the figure of a local haunted house, to which we shall return. Indeed, Carpenter confirms that the urban legend of 'The Hook' was a formative influence on *Halloween* (author interview). On November 8, 1960, Abigail 'Dear Abby' Van Buren printed a letter from 'Jeanette,' reading:

> Dear Abby: If you are interested in teenagers, you will print this story. I don't know whether it's true or not, but it doesn't matter because it served its purpose for me: A fellow and his date pulled into their favourite 'lovers lane' to listen to the radio and do a little necking. The music was interrupted by an announcer who said there was an escaped convict in the area who had served time for rape and robbery. He was described as having a hook instead of a right hand. The couple became frightened and drove away. When the boy took his girl home, he went around to open the car door for her. Then he saw—a hook on the door handle! I don't think I will ever park to make out as long as I live. I hope this does the same for other kids. (qtd. in Brunvand, 1981: 48-9)

The couple come out of it better in this telling than many others, where they are found murdered in some grotesque arrangement or another (often ritualistically arranged, rather as Michael does to the corpses of Annie, Lynda and Bob in *Halloween*). 'The Hook' is perhaps the most famous and enduring of 'teen horror' legends, and it is easy to see the influence on *Halloween*: the semi-rural setting, the unseen, unmotivated killer, the ignored warning, and the interest in teenage sexuality, with a similar (mock?) moralistic aura. The conceptual space of the urban legend grants *Halloween* many of its narrative particulars, but also informs its tone. Kim Newman is correct to write that '*Halloween* seems to be set in a conventional, realistic small town, but actually it takes place in a poetic fantasy world somewhere between the B picture and the fairy tale, where different natural laws obtain' (2011: 201). We can add that it takes place within that grim strain of modern American folklore, where danger lurks within the everyday and cruel coincidences take on cosmic dimensions.[11]

Halloween also evokes a related practice that anthropologists and folklorists have dubbed 'legend tripping' or ostension, where children or adolescents pay clandestine visits to a site of local significance as a dare or a rite of maturity. According to Michael Kinsella, 'A legend trip involves a journey to a specific location and or the performance of certain prescribed actions that, according to local legend, have the potential to elicit a supernatural experience' (2001: 28). Legend tripping is often connected with illicit drinking and drug use, as well as adolescent sexuality. Often considered harmless, legend tripping can pass over into darker terrain, including vandalism and even violence. We see the three boys who had previously bullied Tommy attempt this on the Myers house, Haddonfield's requisite haunted house, before they are chased away by Loomis (one of the film's most amusing moments). In a way, we can think of Michael Myers as being on a legend trip of his own, revisiting the site of his prior murder (the Myers house), collecting a talisman relevant to the crime (Judith's tombstone), and ultimately trying to re-enact the events of fifteen years prior.[12]

It is not hard to see parallels between legend tripping and horror movie spectatorship, especially when the latter is seen as a sexually-tinged rite of passage for youth … the cliché of younger children daring each other to look at the screen, or a teenage boy taking a girl to a horror movie to reap the benefits of her heightened stimulation. Better than perhaps any other film, *Halloween* evokes urban legends and legend tripping to give us the feeling that we are engaged in one even as we watch it. Perhaps this is part of the reason why the film lends itself so well to being watched and rewatched. *Halloween*'s effectiveness stems from its willingness to be basic and elemental, like a campfire story that stays chilling no matter how many times you tell it.

FOOTNOTES

1. Carpenter was of the first generation of horror fans to see the older works principally through television; it seems significant that he puts children in front of the television watching classics. Another example would be *Targets* (1968) by Peter Bogdanovich, another New Hollywood director prone to revisiting and reworking older generic traditions.
2. The very same dead leaves, each time meticulously saved by the crew for the next scene.
3. To the best of my knowledge, Brickman (2012) is the only scholar to explore the sibling angle in any depth.
4. This film cycle has also been dubbed 'stalker' (Dika 1990), 'slash and gash' (Ryan and Kellner 1988) and 'teenie kill pic' (Wood 1986).
5. This is hardly a technique invented by *Halloween*; as William Rothman notes, it can be seen at least as early as Hitchcock's first film, *The Lodger* (1927) (albeit there representing the perspective of a character wrongly assumed to be the murderer) (2004: 79). Rouben Mamoulian used it extensively in *Dr. Jekyll and Mr. Hyde* (1931), and there are many other examples.
6. Ben Singer notes parallels between the Final Girl and the 'serial queens' of silent melodrama: powerful, active and brave female protagonists who are nonetheless frequently subject to fetishistic torments (2001: 222).
7. This is perhaps the most criticized aspect of Clover's formulation of the Final Girl; for one example see Creed (1993: 127). Nowell also notes the presence of many slasher films that do not conform neatly to Clover's model (2011: 167). Sources on the slasher film and the Final Girl not otherwise cited in this book include Rathgeb (1991), Trencansky (2001), Gill (2002), Gentner (2006) and Connolly (2007).
8. As wrong as it may be to conflate the character and the director, there is a very real slippage between Carpenter and Michael Myers, just as there is between Hitchcock and his villains, through the question of showmanship. As Adam Lowenstein notes, 'It's important to remember that it is not just Carpenter outside of the film but Michael within the film who orchestrates these attractions' (2012: 171), such as the three arranged corpses that Laurie finds on the top floor of the Wallace house.

9.   Admittedly, Debra Hill and Moustapha Akkad do the same in the making-of documentary
      Halloween: A Cut Above the Rest.

10.   For another source on the links between the slasher film and urban legends, see Schechter
      (1998: esp. 147-54). The films *Urban Legend* (1998) and *Urban Legends: Final Cut* (2000) pursue
      these connections as well.

11.   Stephen King also links *Halloween* to 'The Hook' in his non-fictional exploration of the horror
      genre, *Danse Macabre* (1981: 34)

12.   Oddly, out of all of *Halloween*'s sequels, this legend tripping theme is most clearly reinforced
      in the unloved *Halloween: Resurrection* (2002), in which the Myers house is the location of a
      horror reality show broadcast live onto the Internet.

CHAPTER 1: *HALLOWEEN*: HOW IT CAME INTO THE WORLD

Despite the fact that the canon of American independent cinema has tended to exclude or marginalise horror films (Sexton 2012), they have been an attractive prospect to independent filmmakers since at least the 1930s. It is no secret why: horror films are generally relatively inexpensive to make and can attract an audience in the absence of a big-name star. Furthermore, a horror film can serve as a calling card, a basic test of competence and technical skill, for a young independent film-maker aiming to capture the attention of the studios. In the decade before *Halloween*, this was proved again and again, especially through films like George A. Romero's *Night of the Living Dead* (1968), Wes Craven's *The Last House on the Left* (1972), Brian De Palma's *Sisters* (1973), Bob Clark's *Black Christmas*, Tobe Hooper's *The Texas Chain Saw Massacre* and David Cronenberg's *Shivers* (1975). This body of innovative low-budget horror films ran alongside (and occasionally intersected with) higher budget, glossier studio productions like *Rosemary's Baby* (1968), *The Exorcist* (1973), *Jaws* (1975), *Carrie* (1976) and *The Omen* (1976). If the first half of the 1930s represented the true Golden Age of the American horror film, the (long) 1970s almost matched its productivity and creativity. In fact, some accuse *Halloween* of spelling the end of the '70s horror boom, including its own producer, Irwin Yablans: 'They congratulated me, but I told them: "Fellas, it's over" … When the studios see how much money you can make with this kind of film, they are going to want to get in on the action, and then you will be finished, and that's what happened' (Zinoman 2011: 189).

John Carpenter's name appears above the title on *Halloween* (a condition that the business-savvy young film-maker extracted from the producers), but the project existed before he came on board. Yablans rightly claims the mantle of 'The Man Who Created Halloween', the title of his 2012 autobiography. An experienced independent film producer and distributor, Yablans had co-founded Compass International Pictures in 1976 and was looking to make a low-budget horror film with youth appeal, following the example of *Black Christmas*, but also inspired by *Psycho* and *The Exorcist*. As Yablans tells it, he conceived the idea after returning from the 1976 Milan Film Festival, where he was exhibiting Carpenter's film *Assault on Precinct 13* (1976):

As the plane winged over the blackness below, I pondered how I could emulate that successful formula for a movie that Carpenter might want to direct for Compass as a follow-up to *Assault*. The idea came to me that a movie about babysitters in jeopardy could be interesting. I reasoned that everyone had either been a babysitter, hired one, or at very least, been a baby. It all flowed so effortlessly in the darkness of that first-class cabin. I thought: let's set the story on one night and one location to control the budget. Both *Psycho* and *The Exorcist* had benefitted from claustrophobic atmospheres—actually one haunted house, if you will. Suddenly, the eureka moment, the light bulb above my head lit up … yes, an epiphany! Why not set the movie on the night that celebrates fright, Halloween! Hell, why not … let's just call it *Halloween!* (2012: 167)

Yablans must be slightly collapsing the timeline, since Carpenter told me that the project reached him with the tentative title *The Babysitter Murders* before it became *Halloween* shortly thereafter; but Carpenter is still quick to credit Yablans for conceiving the title and the concept. Yablans was also amazed to discover that no previous film had used the tempting name.[13]

Though neither *Assault* on *Precinct 13* nor Carpenter's earlier feature, the cult science fiction comedy *Dark Star* (1974), had been successes in the United States, they had both achieved strong reviews and some financial success in the United Kingdom and Europe. Yablans had faith in the skills of the young graduate of USC's film program, who had repeatedly demonstrated the ability to do wonders with a small budget. Carpenter's student film *The Resurrection of Broncho Billy* (1970), about an urban youth obsessed with Westerns and who experiences everything through the frame of a Western, had even won the Academy Award for Best Short Subject in 1971.[14] *Captain Voyeur*, an earlier student film of Carpenter's that was made during the second year of his program in 1969, was rediscovered in the archives of USC in 2012 and has attracted some interest. It is a black and white short that features a man stalking a woman while wearing a World War II era Arctic ski mask: when I asked Carpenter if it was an early working-through of the themes he would revisit in *Halloween, The Eyes of Laura Mars* (1978)[15] and the TV movie *Someone's Watching Me!* (1978), he said: 'Absolutely no. I know it sounds good but no' (author interview). He regards *Captain Voyeur* as a student work of little value, and in fact urged me not to watch it.

Yablans was partnered with Moustapha Akkad, the Syrian-American film producer and the director of the controversial Mohammed biopic variously released as *Mohammed: Messenger of God* and *The Message* (1976), which Yablans had distributed in North America. Akkad would become the man most responsible for keeping the *Halloween* franchise alive in the subsequent decades, but at the time he was essentially a silent partner. Akkad was too busy prepping his expensive biopic of the Libyan patriot Omar Mukhtar, funded in large part by the government of Muammar Gaddafi and released in English as *Lion of the Desert* (1981), to take much direct interest in the production of *Halloween* (Yablans, 2012: 172–3). He would tragically die in 2005, a victim of the Amman terrorist bombings in Jordan; his son Malek Akkad has acted as a producer on subsequent *Halloween* films. Convinced by Yablans of the feasibility of the project, Akkad put forward *Halloween*'s $300,000 budget. Carpenter agreed to direct the film with some bold conditions: that he would have complete creative control, that he would get ten per cent of the net profits, and would get to compose his own score.

On several occasions, *Black Christmas* director Bob Clark has claimed to have had a minor hand in inspiring *Halloween*. One such occasion was in a Q&A held after a screening of *Black Christmas* in Santa Monica's Nuart Theatre, in December 2004 (included as a special feature on the DVD release of the film). When asked by an audience member if it was true that he had planned a sequel set on Halloween, Clark acknowledged that this was a sore spot. He describes working on a project with Carpenter set in 'the Tennessee mountains with retarded people'. This was *Prey*, an ultimately unproduced film that Carpenter scripted and Clark was slated to direct. In Clark's telling, Carpenter, whom Clark described as a 'big fan of *Black Christmas*', asked Clark if he was going to do a sequel, and Clark replied that no, he had no further interest in making horror films. Carpenter asked 'If you did do it, what would it be?' and Clark said: 'I would have it that the killer was caught, it's later that year, the next fall, and he has escaped, and he's going back to the sorority house, and I'm going to call it *Halloween*.' Clark holds short of accusing Carpenter of ripping him off, adding: 'But let me say this. John Carpenter wrote a screenplay, directed the movie, cast it, did the music, edited, did all of that, and in fact the movie was brought to him by the company with the title already on. So I think John loved [*Black Christmas*] and I believe he was interested some by it, but he did not copy my movie and *Halloween* is entirely John

Carpenter's and it's one of the greats.' When I asked Carpenter about this story, he confirmed the key details, including that the films had nothing in common beyond being set on Halloween night; since Clark's 2007 death, however, Carpenter has been vocal about the fact that he was not particularly fond of *Black Christmas* and mainly saw it as an example of what *not* to do.

When asked what went through his mind when he first heard that the project was called *Halloween*, Carpenter says:

> Well you know, I thought, 'Well I can do that. That's a fun idea.' Halloween for me was always a beloved holiday, I really enjoyed it and I just thought it was a really good idea. Back at the time I was just trying to get a career going in the movie business so it wasn't until I started working on the screenplay, did some of these themes that you see in *Halloween*, start coming to bear but at first, it was a work for hire. I was just delighted by it, it was great, we can do something with this. (author interview)

Carpenter brought Debra Hill, his script supervisor on *Assault on Precinct 13* and his romantic partner at the time, onto *Halloween* as a producer and co-writer. After some preliminary conversations, Carpenter busied himself with shooting *Someone's Watching Me!*, leaving Hill to complete the first draft of the screenplay. Her contribution to the film is incalculable. The film's setting is named after Haddonfield, New Jersey, where she grew up,[16] and among her writing contributions was the dialogue between Laurie, Annie and Lynda, the authentic ring of which helps gives the film the sense of verisimilitude that elevates it above many of its followers. While Hill focused on the girls, Carpenter's writing focused on Dr. Loomis and Michael Myers; in fact, it is tempting to see their authorial voices melding in *Halloween*, with Hill's writing anchoring it in the everyday while Carpenter pitched it into the cosmic.

The scriptwriting process was smooth, and the film began casting. Though not Carpenter's first choice, Jamie Lee Curtis was an ideal piece of casting as Laurie Strode, in part because of her parentage. Having the eighteen-year-old daughter of Janet Leigh and Tony Curtis in the lead had publicity value: 'I found a shot of Janet Leigh in the infamous shower scene from *Psycho* and placed it alongside one of Jamie, in a similar screaming pose. We sent it out on the wires, and it made every newspaper in the country' (Yablans, 2012: 171).[17] The film's status as a descendent of *Psycho* is also signified by the character name Sam Loomis, borne by John Gavin's character in *Psycho*.[18] The film's budget was raised slightly to between $320-325,000[19] to accommodate the paycheque of Donald Pleasence, to whom the part of Dr. Loomis was offered once Christopher Lee and Peter Cushing declined. By all accounts, Pleasence was a prickly but not obstructive presence among the young cast and crew, giving the role all of the professionalism it required despite only being on set for five days.

The film was shot out of sequence to accommodate Pleasence's schedule and took twenty-one days overall, with the technically demanding opening sequence filmed last. Locations were chosen around L.A., principally in South Pasadena, that could substitute for the film's small town setting – architecture with the proper look, wide streets, and a minimum of palm trees (but, as noted, some of those sneak into the frame nonetheless). Even pumpkins were hard to come by in March. In a well-known bit of trivia, the subsequently iconic Michael Myers mask was a Captain Kirk mask, which bore only the most passing resemblance to William Shatner to begin with, repainted and modified to fit the 'pale, neutral features of a man weirdly distorted by the rubber' described in the screenplay. Production designer Tommy Lee Wallace describes purchasing the Kirk mask alongside a clown mask. Though the latter choice might have lined up well with Michael's clown getup in the prologue, Carpenter says that it was never seriously in consideration for him (author interview).

The film wrapped on time and on budget. The most significant postproduction element was its influential score by Carpenter, which he composed and recorded in two days. Carpenter maintains he did it himself merely to save time and money, though one suspects a certain false modesty there: the film is now unthinkable without its score. Carpenter is the son of composer and music professor Howard Ralph Carpenter and he maintained a sideline as a musician for many years, fronting several jazz and rock bands as well as mostly composing the scores to his own films.[20] While the minimalist and primitivist *Halloween* score was clearly influenced by music from *Psycho*, *The Exorcist* and Dario Argento's films, it is as distinct as any of those. Carpenter has said that the 5/4 time that dominates the main theme was something he learned from his father when given a set of bongo drums. As Carpenter puts it, '5/4 is nuts, you know, where does it end and what's going on? You can't find the start and stop of it; it's off' (qtd. in Burnand and Mera 2004: 59). Despite the fact that the piece can be organised into standard four-measure phrases, an unevenness is created in terms of the repetitions of certain phrases, as well as how on Carpenter stays on each chord. The piece is dominated by a rhythmic ostinato that continually sequences through a number of minor chords, destabilising any sense of tonal certainty

Yablans sold its overseas rights at the Milan Film Festival and then decided to open it discreetly at a lone theatre in Kansas City, where it broke records. It was subsequently released in Chicago in three drive-ins, an undesirable run for which Yablans negotiated a 90/10 contract in favour of Compass. Mild weather ensured success for the film's Chicago release, and it also led to positive reviews from Gene Siskel and Roger Ebert, local but publically syndicated critics, who would later praise the film on their television show. This and subsequent positive reviews in New York cemented the film's critical acclaim, with Carpenter being hailed as a promising new auteur. Dave Kehr of the *Chicago Reader* compared Carpenter favourably to an earlier generation of film-makers, even locating him as a kind of missing link between the classic and New Hollywoods:

> Eschewing the higher flights of self-expression encouraged by Altman and Company, Carpenter belongs to the oldest and, I think, finest tradition of American film-making, putting the audience first and letting his own quirks enter only later. As a director, he prefers invisibility over the stylistic intrusions favoured by most junior auteurs; his editing has the same subliminal smoothness developed by Ford and Hawks. (2011: 72)

Many *would* compare the film to Hitchcock and *Psycho* in particular, a comparison it obviously courted. Ebert stated plainly: '*Halloween* is an absolutely merciless thriller, a movie so violent and scary that, yes, I would compare it to *Psycho*' (2007: 312, original emphasis).

The critical acclaim was hardly universal. *The New Yorker*'s influential critic Pauline Kael, for one, damned it with faint praise: 'Maybe when a horror film is stripped of everything but dumb scariness—when it isn't ashamed to revive the stalest device of the genre (the escaped lunatic)—it satisfies part of the audience in a more basic, childish way than sophisticated horror pictures do' (1979: 178). Similarly, Jonathan Rosenbaum located it in a genre called he dubbed 'the Mainstream Simulated Snuff Movie . . .or MSSM for short', which 'operates according to two fast and disgusting rules: suspense is generated by an audience waiting for a woman to be torn apart by a maniac, and the act is "morally" prepared for – unconsciously sanctioned – by identifying her with illicit sex.' Though he praises Carpenter's craft, he wonders 'What is he (and are we) honouring in the MSSM, and what makes this morally superior to fondling Nazi war relics?' (1979: 8-9). This review laid some of the foundations for future critiques of *Halloween*.

Yablans' marketing and distribution ingenuity played a large role in securing *Halloween*'s success but it went far anyone's expectations, reportedly making back its original budget sixty-fold in its initial release alone. Many, many sources claim that it was the most profitable independent film of all time, at least until displaced by another horror film, *The Blair Witch Project* (1999). This stems from an inaccurate claim made in the *New York Times* in 1979 (Nowell, 2011: 110), but the point stands that *Halloween*'s success was vast and perhaps unprecedented among independent horror films.[21] Explaining (let alone replicating) the success of a 'sleeper hit' is always difficult, but it seems apparent that *Halloween* was uniquely positioned to benefit from overlapping currents in the New Hollywood, the American independent cinema, 'youth cinema' and the horror film. And yet *Halloween*'s success cannot be strictly reduced to good timing, either. It has proved to be a perennial favourite.

Halloween was also well positioned to benefit from a new wave of academic interest in the horror film. In the 1960s and '70s, the youthful field of Film Studies was aggressively establishing itself on North American campuses, and throughout the '70s became more interested in the study of film genre. If the Western – cinema's, or at least Hollywood's, genre of genres – was perhaps the first cinematic genre to receive concerted study, horror would be second. In 1979, The Festival of Festivals, to be renamed the Toronto International Film Festival fifteen years later, hosted a retrospective of horror films called 'The American Nightmare', which showcased newer work by directors like David Cronenberg, George A. Romero, Larry Cohen and Brian de Palma. 'The American Nightmare' was co-curated by the famed critic and University of Toronto professor Robin Wood. A hundred-page booklet was distributed at the festival, also going by the title *The American Nightmare*, which is now regarded as the first collection of academic essays on horror films. It included essays by Wood, Richard Lippe, Tony Williams and Andrew Britton, turning the semiotic/Marxist/psychoanalytic mélange that broadly characterised 1970s film theory to the horror film, arguing for an understanding of horror deeply linked with repression (sexual or otherwise).[22] Though Carpenter, unlike some of the directors listed above, did not participate in the festival, he knew and admired Wood's writings on film-makers like Hitchcock and Howard Hawks (though he disagreed with the homosexual subtext Wood found in Hawks's works), and told me that Wood even sent him a copy of one of his essays on horror films (author interview). In the seminal essay 'An Introduction to the American Horror Film', Wood's discussion of *Halloween* falls under a section called 'The Reactionary Wing', though he stresses that if *Halloween* is not strictly reactionary, it is only because it is 'confused':

> it clearly wants to be taken, on a fairly simple level, as a 'progressive' movie, notably in its depiction of women. What it offers on this level amounts to no more than a 'pop' feminism that reduces the whole involved question of sexual difference and thousands of years of patriarchal oppression to the bright suggestion that a woman can do anything a man can do (almost). This masks (not very effectively) its fundamentally reactionary nature. (1979a: 26–7)

Wood also notes that 'Carpenter's interviews … suggest that he strongly resists examining the connotative level of his own work; it remains to be seen how long this very talented film-maker can preserve this false innocence' (1979a: 26). When asked about this, Carpenter assured me that he never had false innocence, but was *really* innocent, working instinctively rather than intellectually, though his film-making would become more reflective over time (author interview). Wood's essay helped establish the understanding of *Halloween* as a misogynistic text that would be at turns supported, questioned and complicated by a variety of later scholars. Other important treatments would follow by Steve Neale in 1981 and J.P. Telotte in 1987; not just key essays on *Halloween* but important contributions to the general study of cinematic horror. If *Halloween* would swiftly become a canonical horror film in the minds of the public and an influential one for a generation of film-makers, it quickly took its place in Film Studies too, and remains a mainstay of horror classes.

THE EXTENDED EDITION

Many are unaware of the existence of an extended edition of *Halloween*. The DVD of the extended edition released by Anchor Bay is now a valuable rarity. (The 2013

Blu-ray release includes the new scenes from the extended edition as special features, but the Anchor Bay extended edition release is the only place to see this footage integrated into the film.) This version stems from the October 1981 television debut of the film, where NBC asked for additional material to bring it up to broadcast length (two hours, included commercials). Carpenter, just finished with *Halloween II* and doing preproduction on *The Thing* (1982), complied, though he found it an unhappy task and dismisses the additional scenes as 'simply filler' and 'completely unnecessary ... [they] just slowed it down' (author interview). The new scenes were shot during the production of *Halloween II* and comprises roughly twelve minutes of new footage including the following sequences:

- Two court psychiatrists read out a decree remanding 'Michael Audrey Myers' (curious middle name!) to the Smith's Grove Sanitarium, and declare that he will be tried as an adult on turning 21 for the murder of his sister.[23] Dr. Loomis objects, saying that Michael should not be held in a minimum-security facility. He is convinced, after six months of observing Michael, that Michael is highly dangerous and merely 'covering up ... this catatonia is a conscious act. There's an instinctive force within him. He is waiting'. For what, Loomis cannot say. The court psychiatrists pay him no heed, and offer to replace him as Myers's doctor. Loomis says, 'I'll stay with him'.

- Immediately after this, Loomis goes and visits Michael in his cell, where he sits silently and looks out the window. This child version of Michael looks more than six months older than when we see him in the opening sequence, and has much lighter hair than either Will Sandin or Tony Moran. Loomis says 'You've fooled them, haven't you, Michael? But not me'. Pleasence's delivery of the line is, by a wide margin, the best part of the additional material.

- The second sequence follows Laurie's visit to the porch of the Myers house. Loomis storms through the hallways of Smith's Grove with a nurse, witnessing the chaotic aftermath of Michael's escape. She tells him that most of the escaped patients have been rounded up, but that she does not know how Michael escaped. Michael's cell is littered with debris. The nurse shows him the word 'SISTER' carved onto the back of the door.

- After the scene where Laurie sees Michael from her second floor bedroom, Lynda comes by her house. Urging Laurie to shut the door quickly, she says that she is being followed by the station wagon they saw on the street earlier. Lynda thinks the stalker is someone named Steve Todd. When Laurie says she saw him staring at her from the classroom, Lynda is incredulous ('Steve Todd was staring at you?'), and doubly so after Laurie says that he thinks he was in her back yard. As it transpires, Lynda is here to borrow Laurie's silk dress for her date with Bob. The phone rings, and it is Annie asking after the same dress. Laurie lends it Lynda, and once she's alone she looks out at the street and sings 'I wish I had you all alone, just the two of us', the same as she did in an earlier scene. Laurie has her hair in a towel in this sequence, reputedly because Jamie Lee Curtis's hairdo no longer matched continuity.

While these additional sequences are interesting to see for a fan of the film, none of it is particularly vital. Now when we see Dr. Loomis arguing with Dr. Wynn and insisting that he had told everyone that the security was not equal to containing Michael, we know exactly what he means ... but was it ever important? Likewise, we know now that the dress Lynda is so concerned about Bob tearing is borrowed from Laurie, but does that matter?[24] The sequence about the dress reinforces the point that Laurie is put-upon by her friends (as well as so socially repressed that she has not yet worn the dress) but actually makes Annie and Lynda a shade less sympathetic in the process.

Perhaps of greatest interest is the fact that we see Loomis acting rather antagonistically towards Michael in this version from less than a year after Judith's murder. This rather casts doubts upon his noble claim that he spent the first eight years trying to help Michael, and buoys the theory that Loomis has contributed to Michael's psychosis through systematic abuse. Of course, the presence of the word 'SISTER' on Michael's door alludes to the siblinghood of Michael and Laurie far more strongly than anything in the original cut of *Halloween*. Rather perversely on Carpenter's part, it also denudes *Halloween II* of its big surprise.

FOOTNOTES

13. For a good overview of the role Halloween had played on screen before 1978, see Skal (2002: 155-161).

14. Carpenter is sometimes described as an Oscar-winning film-maker on this basis, but though he wrote, edited and scored the film, the director of record was James R. Rokos.

15. Carpenter wrote the original screenplay as *Eyes*, but the finished film was changed vastly from his initial conception.

16. The real Haddonfield is otherwise most famous as the site of the discovery of the first fully intact dinosaur, a hadrosaurus, in 1848.

17. For a discussion of Curtis's star presence as working to gentrify the film's reputation, see Nowell (forthcoming).

18. Similar tributes are everywhere in *Halloween*, and speak both to the film's self-reflexive tendencies and an auteurist impulse to plant in-jokes, naming characters after colleagues and friends. The name of the nurse, Marion Chambers, combines Marion Crane (Janet Leigh) and Deputy Sheriff Chambers (John McIntire) from *Psycho*. The sheriff is named Leigh Brackett in tribute to the (female) science fiction novelist and screenwriter, Tommy Doyle for a character in *Rear Window* (1954), and Michael Myers' name comes from the British distributor of *Assault on Precinct 13*. The only-mentioned character Ben Tramer (who dies ignominiously in *Halloween II*) is named for a friend of Carpenter's, and the Wallace family are named for Tommy Lee Wallace. It has been claimed that Laurie Strode is named for an ex-girlfriend of Carpenter, but he tells me that this is a myth and he cannot recall the inspiration for the name.

19. Sources differ on this minor point.

20. At the time of *Halloween*, he played in a band called The Coupe DeVilles with his regular collaborators Nick Castle and Tommy Lee Wallace. The Coupe DeVilles would provide the diegetic score for *The Fog* and are even mentioned in dialogue in that film, and later released a promotional video for Carpenter's film *Big Trouble in Little China* (1986).

21. This claim is repeated in publicity material related to *Halloween* until this day: the 2007 Blu-ray release declares it as 'The most successful independent motion picture of all time' in bold letters.

22. See Lowenstein (2012: 154-5) for an account of the Festival's importance.

23. Presumably, this is why Dr. Loomis and Nurse Chambers are collecting Michael in 1978.

24. Why, then, does Lynda say, 'It's expensive' rather than 'It's borrowed'? Perhaps she does not want Bob to know it is borrowed.

CHAPTER 2: THE HAUNTING OF HADDONFIELD

Michael Myers is not a ghost. That much ought to be obvious. As Phil Hardy writes, 'Despite all the talk of the bogeyman … there is nothing of the supernatural in the film. [The killer] is a creature of flesh and blood who bleeds when stabbed, who can be stopped by bullets, yet who obstinately refuses to die' (1986: 329). Be that as it may, there is nonetheless much of the classic ghost story about *Halloween*, and much of the ghost in Michael. On the Laserdisc audio commentary for *Halloween*, Debra Hill even states, 'This is a haunted house movie. There's no question about it'. Carpenter shares this impression, noting that a key element of the film's initial conception was the fact that: '[e]very small town, it seems, has a house where something happened, considered to be haunted … we had one in my small town. It was out on so-and-so road, supposedly haunted or something awful happened there, you know it's an old idea, and I thought, well, I could take something and make something out of this and it's kind of an American gothic kind of movie' (author interview).

It may not be surprising that Carpenter next tackled a ghost story in his underrated *The Fog* (1980), a film that shares much with *Halloween*. The two films have some of the same key personnel in front of and behind the camera (Jamie Lee Curtis, Nancy Loomis and Charles Cyphers, as well as cinematographer Dean Cundey, editor Tommy Lee Wallace, art director Craig Stearns and a host of others). The share the setting of a small American town with a dark curse: in *The Fog*, Antonio Bay, California, turns out to have been founded by murderers who rigged the shipwreck of a load of lepers and stole their gold. One hundred years later to the day, they return from the sea in the form of a glowing, roiling fog to take six lives – stand-ins for town founders who conspired to rob and murder them. It is tempting to think of *The Fog* and *Halloween* as companion pieces, Carpenter's twin haunting narratives. This chapter argues that, formally, narratively and thematically, Michael is constructed as a haunted force, and Haddonfield as a haunted space.

THE TODOROVIAN MICHAEL MYERS

One common framework for dealing with the supernatural in literature (and less directly, film) comes from the Bulgarian structural narratologist Tzvetan Todorov. In his 1970 book *The Fantastic: A Structural Approach to a Literary Genre*, Todorov delineated three modes for the literary supernatural: the Marvellous, the Uncanny and the Fantastic. The Marvellous depicts a world that is certainly different from ours, in which things that are supernatural to us are definitive facts. This includes the fantasy worlds of *Gulliver's Travels*, *The Lord of the Rings* or *A Song of Ice and Fire*, but also perhaps works like *Eternal Sunshine of the Spotless Mind* (2004), taking place in a world that appears to be our own but with minor, significant differences. The Uncanny is perhaps the most difficult to define of the three (and not just because this use of 'uncanny' is quite different from the more familiar uncanny of Freud; some scholars prefer to render Todorov's *l'etrange* as 'strange' instead [Gunning, 2008: 71]): it depicts a world that is different from ours but in a way that is not supernatural in nature, but simply strange. The Fantastic, on the other hand, is based on hesitation, on forcing the reader (and very often, one or more characters too) to vacillate between natural and supernatural explanations. The ghost stories authored by the Edwardian great M.R. James are often described as paradigms of the literary Fantastic, being carefully constructed to allow the reader to believe that the supernatural events are real or that they are hoaxes, delusions, etc. James's principle was that all ghost stories should leave a naturalistic loophole, but that the loophole should be 'small enough to be unusable' (qtd. in Todorov, 1970: 46).

However, Todorov cautions that pure examples of these three modes are less common than narratives that move from one to the other. A Fantastic-Uncanny narrative, for instance, would force the reader to vacillate between natural and supernatural explanations before delivering a naturalistic answer. This is the standard mode of the first wave or 'Radcliffean' gothic, though many today would associate it more heavily with *Scooby Doo*, in which monsters, ghosts and demons are inevitably revealed to be fronts for all-too human villains. In the Fantastic-Marvellous, however, the supernatural ultimately proves to be real; this is almost the default mode for ghost films of recent decades, in which all hesitation and ambiguity eventually gives way to the definitive presence of the supernatural which the characters and the audience must firmly accept.

While Todorov's book does not deal with cinema, other scholars have explored how cinematic techniques can create a Fantastic mode. Noël Carroll uses the example of the spellbinding 'bus scene' in the Val Lewton/Jacques Tournier classic *Cat People* (1942), which implies but does not confirm that Irena (Simone Simon) has transformed into a black panther to stalk her romantic rival. We hear a noise that may well be the roar of panther or the sound of bus; we see movement in the trees that may be where the panther has just leaped, or it may be simply the wind. Carroll writes that cinema 'by means of editing, camera angulation, camera positioning, lighting, pacing (both inside and between shots), object placement, set design, and so on, can problematize any or all of these conditions for knowledge by observation for the spectator' (1990: 155) and achieve a cinematic version of the Fantastic by forcing the audience to hesitate between naturalistic and supernatural interpretations. Many of *Halloween*'s most effective moments similarly depend on Fantastic hesitation.

Fascinatingly, at least two different scholars have applied Todorov's theories to *Halloween* and drawn what might appear to be incompatible conclusions. In the excellent book *The Pleasures of Horror*, Matt Hills draws attention to the limitations of Todorov's model of the Fantastic in literature, including its ahistoricity and its lack of ability to account for differences in viewer perspective: '[W]ould a devout Catholic experience *The Exorcist* (1973) as fantastic-marvellous, or would their interpretation lack any 'fantastic' hesitation due to their religious view of the "laws of the world"?' (2005: 38) He also wonders if there might be a possibility for modes unconsidered by Todorov, including the Uncanny-Fantastic, which would introduce fantastic hesitation only at the *end* of the narrative. For an example of this, Hills points to *Halloween*, which he interprets as an Uncanny narrative throughout most of the film (natural explanations for Michael's crimes being sufficient) that only turns Fantastic in its last moments, when Dr. Loomis looks down from the balcony only to see that Michael has disappeared. Only at this point, suggests Hills, are we given to wonder if Michael is something more than a man, if the supernatural has been in play the entire time.

In contrast, Andrew Patrick Nelson describes *Halloween* as a film in the Fantastic mode, unlike its remake. By introducing clearer psychological explanations for Michael's crimes, giving him a traumatic childhood and a stronger motivation to kill, Rob Zombie's film takes place more in the Uncanny. Writes Nelson, 'Carpenter's film suggests a fantastic hesitation as to the nature of its uncanny events by refusing to provide a tangible explanation for Michael Myers – the origin of his iniquity, the nature of his physical power, the motivation for his murderous actions' (2010: 106).[25] Strangely, despite their different conclusions, I do not find myself in substantial disagreement with either of these scholars. The fact that Hills and Nelson draw such different conclusions about *Halloween*'s place in Todorov's typology is instructive in itself and may (to echo a point made by Hills) merely points to the limitations of using Todorov to discuss certain films, *Halloween* included. If there is some temptation to locate *Halloween* within what Cynthia Freeland (1995) has described as 'realist horror' (see, for instance, Knight and McKnight [2008:, 216]), a tradition that includes *The Texas Chain Saw Massacre, Henry: Portrait of a Serial Killer* (1986) and *The Silence of the Lambs* (1991), much about its themes and its visual style ally it instead with a more supernatural brand of horror. Even if we accept that Michael Myers is no literal ghost, and that, narratively speaking, nothing he does is other than natural and explicable, the aura of the supernatural and the ghostly surrounds him and, in fact, suffuses the entire film.[26]

HAUNTED HOUSES AND LEGEND TRIPS

Walter Kendrick writes that 'If anything holds the scary tradition together, it's the spooky house, which has stood fast for two hundred and fifty years while the world around it has undergone some unimaginable changes' (1991: 69). The archetypical haunted house is incarnated in *Halloween* as the Myers house (referred to in dialogue as the 'old Myers place'), the decrepit ruin that stands so forebodingly on an otherwise bucolic Haddonfield street. The gothic palaces of old reinterpreted within an American vernacular, the haunted house is a repository for terrible secrets the town would rather forget. Carpenter and Hill have both spoken about the presence of such houses in their own hometowns of Bowling Green, Kentucky, and Haddonfield, New Jersey, respectively. All small American towns are meant to have such a thing; haunting is structuring element of what makes a town a town. These sites evolved from the dark houses of Poe and Hawthorne, so often haunted by twisted family dynamics. Despite substantial continental roots, the haunted house story has taken on a special importance in the United States, perhaps because of the central role home ownership takes in the

American dream. Writes Dale Bailey, the haunted house 'is a profoundly versatile tool for examining the anxieties and tensions inherent in our national experiment … [it] seems like nothing less than a symbol of America and the American mind, of all the ghosts that haunted us, from the dark legacy of slavery to the failed war in Vietnam' (1999: 114). Regarding *Halloween*, we might reflect that the murder of Judith Myers takes place a mere twenty-two days before the Kennedy assassination, Haddonfield's loss of innocence being closely allied with the mythical end of American innocence.

Tommy looks warily up at the decrepit Myers house, Haddonfield's local haunted house.

But as James Ellroy says in the first lines of his Kennedy-assassination opus *American Tabloid*, 'America was never innocent. We popped our cherry on the boat over and looked back with no regrets' (1995: 1). Teresa A. Goddu regards the American gothic, a tradition to which we have seen Carpenter explicitly link *Halloween*, as serving precisely to refute the official American mythology of the newness and innocence (1997: 10), and in *Halloween* the Myers house serves as a locus of the gothic's survival in the modern world. In this regard, it is much like the Bates house in *Psycho*: a grim, imposing structure surrounded by everyday banality, a reminder of the past's inexorable haunting of the present. Surprisingly little of the action of *Halloween* takes place at the Myers house, but its importance as a location is such that the film both begins and ends matching with full-frame shots of it. In the years since Judith's murder, it has become the kind of small town haunted house that figures strongly in local lore. The children of the town do not seem to know much about it except that it is a dark and haunted location. Tommy warns Laurie not to go onto the porch of this 'spook house' where something bad once happened. Tommy heard not to go the Myers house from bully Lonnie Elamb,[27] and despite the dubious source this is actually wise advice, since Michael sees her from inside and begins stalking her as a consequence. Sheriff Brackett also tells Loomis that every kid in town thinks of the place as haunted ('They may be right,' says Loomis), and later, Tommy's three bullies, Lonnie, Keith and Richie, visit it on Halloween night, trying to dare each other to go in, classic legend-tripping behaviour.

In his study of legend tripping in Ohio, Bill Ellis discovered that the most popular locations are 'said to be the setting of some gruesome accident, murder, hanging or tragic natural death', and are generally either rural or 'along rural-seeming streets' (1982/3 62), just like in *Halloween*. Lonnie, Keith, and Richie's brief visit (they are chased away by Loomis, who crouches in the bushes and whispers 'Hey Lonnie! Get your ass away from there!') hints at the role the Myers place has taken on in Haddonfield lore as the local haunted house. If Haddonfield's official mythology, as articulated by Brackett, is that it is 'families, children, all lined up in rows, up and down these streets', the Myers house exists as a reminder of how easily this idyllic model of family life and childhood can collapse into violence and chaos.

The second-most common location for legend tripping identified by Ellis is a cemetery, 'with a common motif being the return of the dead to punish those who disturb graves' (ibid.). In his discussion of the motif of disturbed burial, Slavoj Žižek argues that tales of ghosts, zombies, vampires, etc. serve as reminders of the necessity of funerary rites: 'The return of the dead is a sign of a disturbance in the symbol rite, in the process of symbolization; the dead return as collectors of some unpaid symbolic debt' (1991: 23). In *Halloween*, when Loomis and the cemetery caretaker discover that Judith Myers's tombstone is missing, the caretaker (Arthur Malet) immediately attributes the theft to legend-tripping adolescents: 'Goddamn kids! They'll do anything on Halloween.' But the culprit is a different kind of 'kid', Michael himself; this time, the ghost is not unleashed through the disturbance of the grave, but is the one doing the disturbing. We may even think of the disturbance in the cemetery as an act of self-conjuration, Haddonfield's resident ghost doing what is necessary to will himself into being.

Even if Michael has not been in Haddonfield since his crime, in a way he has never left; the Myers house has stood as a silent, decrepit reminder of his inexorable presence in the town's collective self. In the book *Haunting Experiences* (2007), folklorist Sylvia Ann Grider sums up the appearance of an archetypical haunted house from children's stories and drawings as a list of stock elements: 'multistoried, mansard or gambrel roof, turrets or towers, and broken or boarded-up windows with "spooky" inhabitants peeking out' (2007: 147). The Myers house, a modest middle-class locale, lacks the more aristocratic elements but fits in other ways, especially in being multi-level. As such, it also features the staircase that Grider describes as central to a great many ghost stories: 'The liminal staircase … joins the two terminal loci of the attic and basement; being on the staircase means that one is neither up nor down. In oral ghost stories, the general pattern is for the helpless human victim to hide or take refuge in an upstairs bedroom or the attic when the ghost is first heard or appears on the stairs' (2007: 153).

Halloween loves staircases. The opening sequence travels both up and down one in the Myers place. In parallel, Laurie walks up a staircase in the Wallace house only to tumble back down it after being attacked by Michael. The image of Michael heading down the stairs after her is one of the film's most menacing. Laurie travels up one in the Doyle house, only to find herself blocked from going down it by Michael. All three of the houses that figure heavily in *Halloween* (and even Laurie's house, which we only visit briefly) are two storey dwellings with a generally similar layout. It is a visual clue to the non-separation of these locales; if the Myers house, the crumbling and unloved spook house, is the locus of Haddonfield's traumatic past, that past does not stay contained there but infests every house. The montage of static shots that close the film trace the evil back to its source, closing by showing the three houses he visited in reverse order: the Doyle house, the Wallace house and finally the Myers house.

This closing shot also leads us to recall that Laurie is introduced delivering the keys to the Myers house on behalf of her realtor father, and it is in that context that Michael first sees her. For fifteen years, the scene of the crime has been a dilapidated ruin, but now it is being sold. Haddonfield is papering over its past. But shameful and traumatic histories often sleep lightly. Parallels with *The Fog* are instructive here: in that film, the ghosts return one hundred years to the day after the shipwreck to disrupt a ceremony honouring their murderers, while Michael returns fifteen years to the day after his sister's murder to reassert his claim on Halloween. Both are ghosts of the past, whether literally or symbolically. When the film's final shot shows us the Myers house, the Strode

Realty sign takes on an ironic edge. The Myers house is for sale, but to whom can it ever really belong except for Michael?

The film's closing image.

GHOST-VISION

It has been noted that vision and perspective are key themes in *Halloween*, introduced from its first moments with the dolly shot into the pumpkin's glowing eye. Writes J.P. Telotte, 'What Carpenter seems intent on demonstrating is how consistently our perceptions and our understandings of the world around us fall short ... We are conditioned by our experience and culture to see less ... to dismiss from our image contents those visions for which we might not be able to account' (1987: 122). Vision is strongly linked to the modern conception of the ghost. Recent scholarship (Smajic, 2011; McCorristine, 2011; Leeder, 2012) has explored the centrality of the visual to the ghost in both fiction and 'reality'. The ghost story took on its contemporary form in the mid-nineteenth century, alongside a complex rethinking of sight that embedded the classical 'noblest of senses' firmly into the materiality of the human body and within the limits of fallible human perspective. Despite the rarity of seeing actual ghosts (as opposed to be perceiving them audibly or through other, less sensory experiences), ghosts came to exist in the cultural imagination first and foremost as things to be seen, though potentially to be seen more by one's mind than by one's eyes. As McCorristine writes, 'Neither the advent of gaslight nor electric light could banish the ghost from the visual field for the ghost-sight had long been affirmed as being an *interior* visuality in both occultist and psychological discourses' (2011: 6). Similarly, Tom Gunning argues that the nineteenth century saw the rise of a specifically optical version of the uncanny:

> in modernity not only does the optical uncanny become crucial and dramatic (as evident in the development of Fantastic literature), but the modern scientific and technological exploration of vision and optics (such as the proliferation of new optical devices) multiple and articulate the possibilities of the optical uncanny. (2008: 70)

As Gunning indicates, the mode of the Fantastic often emerges in the gap between 'what I think I see' and 'what I know to be true' in the age where seeing is no longer necessarily believing. We see this throughout the early part of *Halloween*, where Laurie continues to see Michael but is unsure of what she is seeing . . . as are we. One of the most ambiguous scenes along these lines is when Laurie looks out of her bedroom window to see Michael standing in the garden, flanked by shroudlike white sheets. Carpenter cuts back from Laurie's face and then back to the garden, now empty. There does not seem to be enough time enough for Michael to run away, and even if there had been, Laurie never breaks her gaze. The moment is an excellent cinematic example of Todorov's Fantastic, and of Gunning's constellation of the optical uncanny. Was Michael there? Was his appearance merely a figment of Laurie's imagination? Is he there and then not: materialising and dematerialising like a ghost? Or some complex combination of all three?

Laurie sees (or hallucinates?) Michael's presence in her back garden.

If ghosts are so often affiliated with vision, that sequence reminds us that ghosts are not just there to *be* seen: they are consummate lookers. Carpenter has spoken about being influenced by a classic ghost film: 'There was a movie called *The Innocents* made in the sixties where the ghosts were standing across a pond, just looking. Doing nothing but looking. There's something arresting about that. It stuck in my mind when making *Halloween*' (Zinoman, 2001: 182).

The still, silent, gazing ghost of The Innocents.

In the scene Carpenter is recalling, there is just one ghost, that of Miss Jessel (in a similar sequence earlier in the film, the ghost of Peter Quint stares down from the top of a tower), but it is easy to see how the scene influenced the presentation of Michael Myers's still, silent, spectatorial menace. Just like Laurie looking down into her backyard, Miss Giddens (Deborah Kerr) sees the ghost looking back at her, and then suddenly Miss Jessel is gone, and both Miss Giddens and the audience are left wondering about the status of what they just witnessed.

We often understand the haunted house as having, through some impossible to define process, merged with the identity of its owner or its most famous occupant. The house, on some level, is alive.[28] Debra Hill reports that the house used as the Myers house in *Halloween* appealed to the film-makers because its front looked like a face. The house is not only anthropomorphised, but critically it is also given a gaze of its own, linked to that of Michael and the staring pumpkin of the opening sequence. Themes of vision are layered on each other almost immediately; the pumpkin gives way to Michael's POV,

The camera placement in the back seat of the car suggests Michael's perspective without being an explicitly subjective shot.

staring at the face-house, staring back. The long take creates tension by ignoring the conventions of the classical Hollywood style, where a point of view shot should rarely go long without a reverse shot. We know that we are seeing from someone's eyes – but whose? This is a common strategy in ghost films, in which unassigned camera movements, unusual camera positions, etc. all imply that we may be seeing through the 'eyes' of someone or something unseen. Carroll identifies a comparable example from *The Changeling* (1980), where a handheld shot, different in style to most anything else in the film, crawls around the house and creates the suggestion that we may be seeing from the ghost's perspective. Writes Carroll: 'The audience sees it. And the audience cannot help postulating that the camera movement *might* represent the presence of some unseen, supernatural force ... The audience cannot know this for sure; but the point of the camera movement is to prompt the spectator into a state of uncertainty in which she is tempted toward a supernatural account' (1990: 155). It is a good example of something common in haunted house films: the use of unassigned camera movement to create a cinematic mode of the Fantastic. Similarly, the formal features of *Halloween* are carefully calculated to construct the aura of the supernatural, even if the script never confirms it.

The floating and unearthly effect created by the Panaglide shots works similarly to as the shot in *The Changeling*. Even in the opening sequence, the gliding feel of the camerawork does not quite seem to suggest normal human perspective, and, as many have noted, the camera position seems higher than a six-year-old child should be, as if floating.[29] The effect is carefully allied with Michael's gaze even when we are not given to suspect that it literally is his gaze. Consider the sequence where Michael briefly grabs onto Lonnie Elamb outside the schoolyard: as Michael studies Tommy, he gets into his car and we watch over his shoulder from the back seat of the car, the uneasy, floating camerawork now suggesting Michael's perspective without explicitly emulating it. Similarly, we briefly see from inside the car as Annie lets Laurie off at the Doyle house and then parks at the Wallace house across the street, and the floating quality of the shot makes us suspect we are seeing from Michael's point of view directly, until we realise that 'we' are actually seated next to him in the passenger seat.

Carpenter pulls this trick again and again. Take the sequence where Lynda and Bob enter the Wallace house, an unbroken take of about a minute that ends with the couple making out on the couch. As the camera pulls back, we briefly wonder if we are seeing from Michael's perspective, only to pull past him, standing there watching them. As Steve Neale writes, 'although point of view is strongly marked, none of the shots in question turn out to be point of view shots in the strict sense' (1981: 27). Allied with but yet not precisely replicating Michael's gaze, the Panaglide shots ultimately become an index of Michael's presence even in sequences where he is not physically present at all. They create the implication that his perspective is unpinned from his body and is as mobile and as invisible as the camera's gaze itself, with which it is so frequently allied. In his essay on haunted house movies, Barry Brummett noted that Jean-Louis Baudry's statement that 'If the eye which moves is no longer fettered by a body, by the laws of matter and time, if there be no assignable limits to its displacement' appears to describe a ghost but in fact describes the viewer of a film (1985: 252-3) and in Michael we find a dark embodiment of this traditional alliance between the camera's gaze, the audience's gaze and ghost-vision.

SOUND MATTERS

This emphasis on the visual aspects of the film threatens to neglect the importance of sound. In *Halloween*, sound works similarly to the Panaglide shots in implying a kind of omnipresence to Michael's presence and perspective. At times Michael resembles a being of the acousmêtre, to borrow Michel Chion's terminology: the character or being who is heard without being associated with a corresponding visual presence on the screen. Acoustmêtric characters are known to the audience principally through their voice, like the Boss in *The Testament of Dr. Mabuse* (1933), the Wizard (Frank Morgan) in *The Wizard of Oz* (1939), Dr. Soberin (Albert Dekker) in *Kiss Me Deadly* (1957) and Mother in *Psycho*; while Michael is obviously voiceless, his presence is often felt through sound rather than (or in addition to) concrete embodiment on the screen. Writes Chion, 'The powers [of the acousmêtre] are four: the ability to be everywhere, to see all, to know all, and to have complete power'; one example he raises is 'the voices of invisible ghosts who move about wherever the action goes, and from whom nothing can be hidden' (1999: 24-5).[30] Michael's auditory signature, the equivalent of his voice, is his heavy breathing, which we first hear as he leaves the Myers house after having murdered Judith. Throughout the film, it serves a similar function, implying his presence in the absence of his visage on the screen. In an interesting contrast to the de-acousmatisation process that Chion describes (1999: 27-9) whereby characters like Soberin or the Wizard or Oz ultimately have their voice pinned to a fragile, fallible body, with Michael we actually have the opposite: the last 'presence' we have of him is his breathing over a montage of locations around Haddonfield. His physical presence has fled the screen and left him invisible, incontestable and omnipresent.

Carpenter's score works similarly to project Michael's presence beyond his body. To borrow a phrase K.J. Donnelly uses to describe the demon in *Night of the Demon* (1957), the music surrounding Michael 'does not merely signify [his] presence, it *is* [his] presence' (2005: 93, original emphasis). Like Chion, Donnelly sees film's aural aspects as possessing profound ghostly potential: 'Film music 'haunts' films, both as ghostly references to somewhere else and something else, and as a mysterious demonic manipulative device' (2005: 22). *Halloween* uses music sparingly; numerous early sequences, such as those of the girls talking, are entirely without music. The score does not develop leitmotifs associated with individual characters but associates itself more fully with Michael himself; it is 'the music of the murderer, Michael Myers, cold, impersonal and relentless with an incessant semiquaver pedal note constantly drawing the music forward' (Burnand and Mera 2004: 60). Frequently the music is heard just before or just as Michael is seen or his handiwork is otherwise demonstrated (as when we, but no characters, see the body of the tow truck drivers). In other sequences from which Michael is absent, it drones ominously and creates tension where it might not otherwise exist; take for instance the brief sequence of Laurie watching trick or treaters while sitting on a street corner, waiting to be picked up by Annie. Already shaken by her glimpses of Michael, the score conveys the impression that he is on her mind, or perhaps even that he is *with her* in an unseen capacity. As Donnelly notes, the film's overall musical impulse is to 'establish a tense atmosphere through drones and ostinati' and then punctuated it with stingers (2005: 102), and it is especially those drones and ostinati, that operate in parallel to the restless Panaglide shots to create the impression that Michael occupies Haddonfield inside and out ... and that he does the same to *Halloween* itself, a haunted film at the level of sight and sound.[31]

PARADOXICAL GHOSTS

Michael secretly watches Annie.

Much of Michael's formal presentation thrives on paradox. He is associated with relentless music, but he is nearly silent. And as much as he is associated with the restlessly moving camera, he is equally associated with stillness, just like the ghost in *The Innocents* that Carpenter cites as an influence. Most of his early appearances in Haddonfield are essentially tableaux; Michael stands still as a statue and *looks*. Consider, for example, the moment when Annie is on the phone with Paul and paces laterally in the foreground of the shot, the camera following her as she does. When the camera moves right, we see Michael standing outside the open door at the back of the frame. It moves left and then right again, and Michael is gone. How different would the impact have been if we saw Michael actually move; rather his entrance into and exit from the frame are both concealed by camera movement. The numerous incidents of 'Michael is there!' 'Michael is gone!' prepare us for the closing sequence, where we see Michael lying on the grass after falling off the balcony, before the inevitable cut back to find the same composition with Michael now absent.

Even when Michael does walk, his movements are generally slow and gliding, graceful. Michael is never seen to run after a victim, but he does not lurch like a Romero zombie or the Universal incarnation of Frankenstein's monster either. One wonders Michael's distinctive gait owes something to the moody and beautiful films of the 1940s' greatest horror producer, Val Lewton, among whose favourite images were 'people moving in a penitential, sleep-walking manner' (Farber, 1998: 49). Like Michael, certain among Lewton's characters, notably Jessica (Christine Gordon) in *I Walked with a Zombie* (1943), do not so much walk as float – like a ghost.

At one memorable moment, the Michael-as-ghost subtext becomes more literal. This is when he dresses up as a ghost, or at least a ghost as interpreted through a child's Halloween costume: the classic sheet over the head. Grider links the sheet ghost back to the wrapping of corpses during times of plague: 'This possible connection between children's ghost stories and the plague is a reminder that even the seemingly most trivial of traditions may, in fact, preserve vestiges of our venerable shared human past' (2007: 114). The image of Michael-as-ghost is one of the film's most memorable, taking the Casper get-up, the sheeted ghost of childhood, and making it terrifying because its childishness is so incongruous with the adult violence and sexuality of the situation that surrounds it. He is impersonating the freshly murdered Bob at this point, and he wears Bob's glasses on the outside of the sheet, one of the film's cleverest details. As Lynda tries to egg him on, flashing him her breasts oblivious of his true identity, she giggles and asks: 'Can I get your ghost, Bob?' But Michael stands there silent, still and unresponsive as her frustration grows. As she goes to phone Laurie, he finally steps forward to strangle her with the phone cord.

Michael-as-Bob-as-ghost.

While Lynda struggles through her last moment, the sheets come off and we see what's underneath. As much as that scene presents Michael as a ghost, it makes it equally clear that he is *not* a ghost: beneath that sheet, he is an embodied, still-masked, physical menace. Perhaps more than any other sequence in the film, it foregrounds the film's master paradox: Michael's embodied and disembodied aspects. Parallels with the ghosts in *The Fog* are once again useful. In that film, the ghosts range from pure immateriality, diffusing about threateningly in the form of the fog itself while linked with the ephemerality of radio signals and shapelessness of the ocean, to embodiment in the form of skeletal beings who carry knives and sickles to brutally dismember their victims.[32] This paradox is also at work in *Halloween*. The veneer of a ghost, the most disembodied of horror archetypes, conceals one of the most embodied, the serial killer. Indeed, there is even something *robotic* about Michael, perhaps due in part to the acknowledged influence of *Westworld* (1973) and its robotic gunslinger (Yul Brynner); we perhaps see this most clearly when Michael returns from unconsciousness in the upper floor bedroom of the Doyle house, sitting up in the back of the frame with an inhuman, mechanical motion.[33] The mesh of the material and the evanescent is a major part of what makes Michael such a compelling figure, as he combines aspects of the robot (physicality without spirit) and ghost (spirit without physicality). Indeed, the contrast is stark between his ghost-white face and the coveralls he wears, which are not only dark in colour but imply manual, physical labour, possibly even suggesting the Frankenstein monster as portrayed by Boris Karloff and its clear proletarian coding.

The moment in *Halloween* that I find the eeriest plays on this uncertain space between materiality and immateriality and comes in the Wallace house, just after Laurie has discovered the bodies of her friends. She sobs next to an open doorway; blue light illuminates her face and light shirt, but the doorway behind her is pitch black. Slowly, subtly, Michael's white mask appears from the darkness, looking at her, seemingly manifesting from nothing like the Cheshire Cat. Perhaps he is simply emerging from his hiding spot, but visually one gets the impression that he is materialising from nothingness. But then he steps forward and swings his butcher knife at Laurie, cutting her shoulder and arm and sending her tumbling over the railing. Michael transitions from ghostly gazer to the embodied serial killer in mere seconds.[34]

Michael emerges from the darkness at the right edge of the frame.

Michael's paradoxical embodiment/disembodiment is reinforced in the film's ending. Having just reaffirmed to Laurie that Michael is indeed the boogeyman, Loomis looks off the balcony to see that Michael's body is gone, in spite of having been shot six times and taken a considerable fall. So where is he now? He is nowhere to be seen, but his presence in felt in all things. We see a montage of all the locations Michael has been in Haddonfield throughout the film, each in an elegant tableau. Meanwhile, the soundtrack is layered with the ostinato-driven theme music associated with Michael and his heavy breathing. We know that he is still alive, but we know something more: that he could be in any of those places, or is in *all of them*. One of the first lines we hear in the film is his sister Judith's 'Michael's around someplace' – indeed.

In the BBC documentary *A History of Horror*, Carpenter reflects on the moment in *Psycho* where Mother appears unexpectedly in the frame to kill Detective Arbogast on the staircase. He says: 'That moment of coming out of nowhere influenced me for *Halloween*. If you establish [that] this guy and you establish that he can be anywhere, then the audience will start to believe he can be anywhere, in any shadow.' In the DVD feature *Halloween: A Cut Above the Rest*, Carpenter goes a step further; in describing the closing montage, he says, '[it] means: he's not only gone, he's everywhere'. Michael Myers can be anywhere, and what's worse, he is *everywhere*. Irrespective of his embodied physicality, he has undergone a ghostlike diffusion into the very atmosphere of Haddonfield, his town, and perhaps Halloween itself … his holiday.

FOOTNOTES

25. Carpenter's comments on *Halloween: A Cut Above* seem to support this understanding: 'This guy is a human but he's more than that. He's not exactly supernatural … but maybe he is. Who knows how he got that way?'

26. Likewise, any attempt to read *The Texas Chain Saw Massacre* as realist horror is complicated by the aura of apocalyptic horror that the film consciously creates, with astrological references spelling doom.

27. Tommy exact words are 'Lonnie Elamb said never to go up there,' advice Lonnie does not follow himself.

28. In a famous anecdote, Roger Corman made certain that Vincent Price delivered the lines 'The house lives! The house breathes!' with appropriate gravitas while filming *The Fall of the House of Usher* (1960), since the executives at American International Picture were wary about the film lacking a monster. Said Corman, 'The house is the monster' (Hutchings, 2004: 34).

29. According to Carpenter, this was a function of technical limitation; they could not get the shot to look natural from a child's height (author interview).

30. For another approach to the ghostliness or uncanniness of film sound, one more specific to the horror film, see Spadoni (2007: esp. 8-30).

31. Perhaps the film's most interesting aural moment comes when Tommy watches Michael carrying Annie's corpse, a moment that is silent other than *Forbidden Planet*'s influential and innovative electronic score, the first of its kind (Leydon, 2006: 61), which does so much to construct the alienness of space in general and the film's unseen monster in particular. This moment not only serves as Carpenter crediting a cinematic and musical predecessor, but also serves to locate Michael as a parallel 'monster from the id'.

32. I develop this reading of *The Fog* in Leeder (2009).

33. One might further suggest that the electronic score enhances Michael's 'robotic' qualities, especially when he is associated with the science fiction sounds of *Forbidden Planet*.

34. Cinematographer Dean Cundey uses the word 'materialises' when he describes how he accomplished this shot technically in the documentary *Halloween Unmasked*. He carefully adjusted the dimmer on the camera to increase the exposure on the mask in the darkness.

CHAPTER 3: 'BLACK CATS AND GOBLINS ON HALLOWEEN NIGHT': *HALLOWEEN* AND HALLOWEEN

The children of Haddonfield innocently trick or treating.

For a film called *Halloween*, there is remarkably little trick or treating depicted in it. The few exceptions take on a special interest as a consequence. Early in the film, Laurie spies a group of children trick or treating in her neighbourhood, dressed in archetypical costumes: an angel, a cowboy, a witch, etc. Laurie stops and smiles at them and utters one of the film's most curious lines: 'Well, kiddo, I thought you outgrew superstition.' On the commentary track, Carpenter himself admits to not really understanding the line, authored by Debra Hill, but adds, 'It sure does work'. It works in large part due to the delivery: Curtis delivers the line wistfully, suggesting that Laurie remains nostalgic for the childhood version of Halloween she has outgrown even as she segues into her adult responsibilities. The second time Laurie watches trick or treaters, while sitting on the street waiting to be picked up by Annie, the uneasy ostinato on the soundtrack and the anxious cutting introduces an element of menace that is echoed in the uneasy look on Laurie's face, since she is now becoming more attentive to Michael's presence in Haddonfield. The idyllic childhood facade of Halloween is beginning to peel off, as if unmasked, revealing something darker underneath. This strategy, in which Halloween imagery moves from nostalgia to darkness and violence, is repeated throughout the film.

Laurie wistfully watches the trick or treaters.

Even before the famous subjective cold open, *Halloween* begins with a song, or rather a chant:

Black cats and goblins and broomsticks and ghosts
Covens of witches with all of their hosts
You may think they scare me
You're probably right
Black cats and goblins on Halloween night
Trick or treat!

A cowbell rings, and for an instant, we are in the nostalgic realm of Halloweens past, when children dressed up in costumes and paraded around their neighbourhood with impunity, hatching their mischievous plans and schemes. Carpenter wrote this chant, modelled on those from his childhood, and Jamie Lee Curtis, Nancy Loomis, P.J. Soles and Debra Hill did the voices (author interview). We hear the authentic 'Trick or treat, trick or treat, give me something good to eat,' later in the film. The nostalgic tone does not last: Michael Myers is revealed to be a child, committing the murder of his sister while wearing a clown costume and the same mask that Judith's boyfriend teased her with as they make out on the couch, pressing its bulbous, phallic nose against her face. Michael's costume reminds one of the old saying that 'there's nothing funny about a clown in the moonlight', attributed to none other than the American cinema's first horror star, Lon Chaney, Sr.

One wonders if Michael Myers, in the diegesis of the film, was one of the unseen trick or treaters we hear chanting over the film's opening moments. Is that why he is costumed as a clown – because he was previously trick or treating with his friends? If so, the chant may represent the only words in the film actually spoken by Michael. It seems very likely that we are meant to think Michael has been trick or treating, perhaps led about the neighbourhood by his sister before Judith ditched her responsibilities to make out with her boyfriend. Or perhaps he was off trick or treating with his friends and has only now returned home, catching her making out. In any event, the mask – perhaps Michael's originally, but repurposed by the boyfriend for foreplay and finally donned by Michael in the commission of the murder of Judith – becomes a figure of the liminal space between childhood and adulthood that is also implied by Laurie's 'outgrowing superstitions' line.

A glowing jack o'lantern sits on the porch of the Myers' place, echoing the primal pumpkin of the title sequence and bearing silent witness to the crime. The film is in love with Halloween imagery and makes great use of it throughout. The small town setting feels right, even necessary; Halloween seems to belong on small town streets scattered with dead leaves, a homey and 'safe' space revealing its ominous underbelly. This chapter argues that Halloween is more than simply a setting in Carpenter's film, but that the film is indeed centrally concerned with the contested meanings of the day when it takes place. The film is a cultural artefact of how Halloween was thought about in the 1970s. In other words, it is not just called *Halloween*. It is *about* Halloween.

Something similar cannot quite be said of *Halloween*'s immediate predecessor, *Black Christmas*. That film successfully mines Christmas imagery for a certain amount of ambience and irony, most memorably in the contrapuntal use of music when children singing 'O Come, All Ye Faithful' conceal the noise of a murder. But on the whole, the fact that the film takes place over Christmas is incidental, only serving to justify the characters' isolation. In the years after *Halloween*, there would be a small cottage industry of holiday-set slasher films: *New Year's Evil* (1980), *You Better Watch Out* (1980), *Prom Night* (1980), *My Bloody Valentine* (1981), *Graduation Day* (1981), *Happy Birthday to Me* (1981), *Silent Night Deadly Night* (1984), *April Fool's Day* (1986) and more. Some neo-slashers, like *Valentine* (2001), revived this trend. Not for nothing did Eli Roth contribute a fake trailer for an '80s slasher named *Thanksgiving* as part of Quentin

Tarantino and Robert Rodriguez's *Grindhouse* (2007), though he was actually beaten to the punch by the Thanksgiving-set slasher film *Home Sweet Home* (1981).

The convention comes about because holidays lend themselves well to the two-part structure of the slasher film, as noted by Vera Dika – a something terrible happened in the past, and at a moment of commemoration years later, it threatens to happen anew (1990: 59). For most of those films, the holiday setting is more formulaic than thematically apt, and probably as contrived to take advantage of a release date as anything else. But this is not the case with Halloween, which engages with fraught space that *Halloween* had become by the late 1970s. Indeed, only a few years later, the Reverend Pat Robertson would say on the October 29, 1982 episode of *The 700 Club*, that:

> I think we ought to close Halloween down. Do you want your children to dress up as witches? The Druids used to dress up like this when they were doing human sacrifice … [Your children] are acting out Satanic rituals and participating in it, and don't even realize it. (Bannatyne, 2011: 217)

Conflating all pre-Christian religious practices with Satanism in a manner typical of the American religious right, Robertson indicates that Halloween is a space of danger, and that danger is precisely located in children dressing up and trying on different identities. The timing corresponded perfectly with paranoia stoked by deaths earlier in the month related to cyanide-tainted Tylenol capsules. Numerous jurisdictions banned trick or treating that year or imposed strict curfews, and candy sales fell by 20 per cent (Rogers, 2002: 20).

The influence of Halloween on the behaviour of children also fell under scrutiny. In 1974, a psychological experiment was done with school children showing that aggressive behaviour increased substantially when Halloween costumes were worn. Run by Scott C. Fraser, it involved having children playing games, some of which required aggression and some of which did not, both of which resulted in tokens that could be exchanged for gifts at the end of the party. The children played both while wearing costumes and without them. The researchers found that, 'Aggression increased significantly as soon as the costumes were worn, more than doubling from the initial base level average. When the costumes were removed, aggression dropped well below the initial base rate'

(Zimbardo, 2004: 30). Even more interestingly, it was reported that, when costumed, the children ceased to care about winning the tokens, even though aggressive behaviour cost them rewards: 'aggression had negative instrumental consequences on winning tokens ... but that costs did not matter when the children were anonymous in their costumes' (ibid.). The object of this experiment was to study the effect of anonymity on children's aggression, and the Halloween regalia served merely as an opportunity to organically place the children in conditions of anonymity. One wonders, however, if the Halloween tradition presented a variable the experimenters did not consider. Were these fascinating results a consequence solely of anonymity itself, or rather a kind of anonymity specific to Halloween? It is a tantalising question – did the children act more aggressively because they wore costumes, or because they wore *Halloween* costumes? Halloween is a time 'when children may play with identity, learning that they can use the mask as the facade of an alternative self' (Paul, 2004: 321), so might it not be the case that the children in Fraser's experiment were able to displace their aggressive behaviour on to alternate social personas that are licensed to act differently due to the holiday?

As much as masking is associated with anonymity, it surely reveals something at the same time as it conceals. Halloween is often constructed as a rare time when the anger and discontentment of children, and indeed their capacity for violence, may be demonstrated. This is the role played by Halloween in Vincente Minnelli's classic musical *Meet Me in St. Louis* (1944), in which the Halloween sequence subtly works to complicate the film's cosy and anodyne treatment of early-twentieth century middle class family life. Tootie Smith (Margaret O'Brien), the archetypical rascally younger sister with a morbid streak – she likes to let her dolls die of romantic diseases and stage their funerals – dresses as 'horrible ghost' and becomes a symbolic murderer. In this depiction of turn-of-the-century Halloween customs, local children rule the street after dark, building a giant bonfire made of old furniture and go around ritualistically 'killing' local citizens by throwing flour on them. Thought of as too young to participate in these faux-violent rituals by most of the children, Tootie decides to prove herself by single-handedly taking on Mr. Braukoff, a local man whom the children accuse of such crimes as poisoning cats, beating his wife with a hot poker and, most damningly, having empty whiskey bottles in his cellar. A long tracking shot follows Tootie as she walks through the warped version of her familiar neighbourhood, before she reaches the Braukoffs' door, faces down the old man and his bulldog, gasps out 'I hate you, Mr. Braukoff!' and tosses flour in his face.

Racing terrified back to the bonfire, Tootie triumphantly shouts 'I killed him!' She is hailed by the community of children as the bravest, the most horrible. Tootie cries, 'I'm the most horrible!' and joins the children in tossing chairs onto the fire. Writes Ernest Mathijs:

> Tootie's adventure captures the essence of the Halloween holiday perfectly. It is a little bit frightening but it is also fun. It is a feast, a flaunting of social taboos, and an exercise in testing one's fears. Halloween tests the boundaries of a community's sense of togetherness and its ability to recognize strangers and predators. Through dressing up we check our capacity to tell true danger from fake scares, and to signal both our friendliness and test that of others. (2011: n.p.)

The sequence hints at something darker, too; both the setting of Halloween and her costume permit Tootie to murder a surrogate parent, just as she will eventually ruin the family of snowmen on her porch in protest of her father's decision to move them to New York City (Wood, 2006: 202–4). Tootie is allowed by Halloween to show her true nature more clearly than usual, and that includes a capacity for violence, even (symbolic) murder. At the heart of the rosy nostalgia of *Meet Me in St. Louis*, we can recognise Tootie as a benign predecessor to Michael Myers.

THE HISTORY AND DANGERS OF HALLOWEEN

Meet Me in St. Louis allows a nostalgic peek at American traditions of Halloween long before the advent of trick or treating. If Halloween nominally traces its roots back to the Celtic harvest festival of Samhain,[35] the line is tangled indeed. As David J. Skal writes, 'contemporary Halloween is a patchwork holiday, a kind of cultural Frankenstein stitched together quite recently from a number of traditions, all fused beneath the cauldron-light of the American melting pot' (2001: 20). Since the new cycle of interest in paganism since the 1960s, Samhain – misunderstood and often mispronounced (it should be 'SOW-un'),[36] – has re-entered the vocabulary. *Halloween* itself makes no overt attempt to tie itself to Halloween's purported ancient roots, but many of its other incarnations do. The novelisation to *Halloween*, credited to Curtis Richards and published in 1979,[37] begins with a chapter set in Celtic Ireland during Samhain, telling the story of a disfigured 15-year-old boy named Enda. He is in love with a king's daughter, and when his rage is unleashed, he jealously murders her and her fiancé at the festival. He is in turn ritualistically killed. The priests curse his soul to 'roam the earth till the end of time, reliving thy foul, and thy foul punishment, and may the god Muck Olla visit every affliction upon thy spirit forevermore' (1979: 5). It is heavily implied that Enda's spirit finds a new host in Michael Myers. The close of the strange Ireland-set prologue provides a fanciful account of Halloween's lineage:

> The celebration of Samhain's eve was transmuted over the centuries. The invading Romans carried the tradition back from the English Isles [sic] with them in the form of the Harvest Festival of Pomona, and the early Christians deemed their celebration Hallowmas. The popes of the Middle Ages consecrated November 1 as All Saints' Day, and All Hallow Even slurred into Halloween as the holiday was transmuted over the next millennium.

> With the coming of modern civilization, the superstitions and traditions of the original festival lost their meaning and vitality. Token recognition could be seen in the custom of lighting candles in jack-o'-lanterns, hanging effigies of witches and goblins outside homes, and playing good-natured pranks that were a feeble cry from the mayhem of the old times. Children paraded about in costumes whose significance had long ago lost their correspondence to the terror of evil that had once gripped the world at the onset of winter. Halloween, like so many of the holidays, had become an empty sham.

> Except that from time to time, the innocent frolic of All Hallow Even was shattered by some brutal and inexplicable crime, and the original spirit of the celebration was brought home to horrified world.[38] Then the people would bolt their doors.

> Scant good it did them . . . and besides, there were always the unwary. (1979: 5–6)

If this exposition has little directly to with *Halloween* the film, it tells us something about how the holiday was thought of in the 1970s in at least three ways. First, it reflects the new appreciation of the pagan underlay to modern western society in general (most famously explored onscreen in *The Wicker Man* [1973]), constructed, confused and oversimplified though it may be.[39] Second, there is an understanding that the 'real', 'legitimate' Halloween is something in the past, and it is now a neutered, over-commercialised holiday becoming increasingly removed from any dangerous and transgressive capacity it might have once held.[40] Lastly, in spite of this, Halloween is still perceived as a potential site of danger.

Sequels to *Halloween* delve deeper into the (real or manufactured) lore of Samhain. The word appears scrawled on a chalkboard in *Halloween II*, which Carpenter co-scripted, prompting this reflection from Loomis, in which real and invented Celtic lore melds with psychoanalysis:

> In order to please the gods, the druid priests held fire rituals. Prisoners of war, criminals, the insane, animals were burned alive. By observing the way they died the druids believed they could see elements of the future. Two-thousand years we've come no closer. Samhain isn't the evil spirits, it's not goblins and ghosts or witches. It's the unconscious mind. We're all afraid of the dark inside ourselves.

Carpenter also produced *Halloween III: Season of the Witch* (1982), the Michael Myers-free sequel that boasts one of the oddest plots of all time: a mad Irish toymaker, having stolen a piece of Stonehenge, plans to use his massively-distributed masks to kill all of America's children on Halloween in order to complete an ancient druidic rite. So resolutely in a different continuity that a television screening of *Halloween* plays a narrative role, it nonetheless anticipates the increasing presence of pseudo-Celtic mysticism in the series. In the sixth of the series, *Halloween: The Curse of Michael Myers*, it is revealed that the 'Cult of Thorn,' a group of neo-druids who secretly run Smith's Grove Sanitarium, had been secretly controlling Michael all along! Again, all of this might seem to have little directly to do with the first *Halloween* film, except insofar as it tells us something of the cultural construction of the holiday and the issues that continue to underpin it till this day.

In order to do understand October 31 as a site of violence and mayhem, especially for the youth, one does not need to reach for paganism or to ancient blood rites. By the 1920s, there was a drive to curb the much more carnivalesque behaviours that the Halloween of the time seemed to be rife with. In its American incarnation, Halloween had once been a night of misrule where the young were temporarily allowed to take over the streets, often leaving expensive vandalism in their wake: 'On a typical Halloween spree in interwar North America, fences were destroyed, signs and gates removed, roads barricaded, trolley cars immobilized, street lighting smashed, and outhouses tipped over' (Rogers, 2002: 78). Writes Lesley Pratt Bannatyne: 'By the 1920s, October 31st mischief became known as "the Halloween problem," and many adults began to question the need for a holiday that encouraged pranks and violence. What began as a good-natured tussle between children and adults on Halloween grew into a somewhat serious battle' (1998, 124). Trick or treating, though descending from various mummering and souling traditions, would be introduced in the late 1930s and became widespread in the '50s. It represented a strategy of containment: 'Insofar as rascality could be tolerated at all, it was better that it be rendered child-like' (Rogers, 2002: 86).[41]

But even if we see trick or treating as the ultimate triumph of consumerism and gluttony over rebellion,[42] it still '[connects] hostility to pleasure, defining a time in which children can vent their own hostile impulses. "Trick or treat" carries with it a threat: we'll punish you if you don't give us what we want' (Paul, 2004: 322). And with the mock-threat implied by 'trick or treat' came more serious, if still exaggerated, dangers of another kind: razor blades, needles and poison in Halloween apples and candy. The most famous case occurred in 1974, when eight-year-old Timothy O'Bryan of Deer Park, Texas died after consuming Pixy Stix laced with cyanide. Yet Timothy's death was not the consequence of some prankster poisoning Halloween candy to sow death and horror among the innocent, but rather from his own father, trying to use that urban legend as a smokescreen for his own crimes: Ronald Clark O'Bryan murdered his son for the insurance money. He was found out quickly, was convicted of first-degree murder and would be executed in 1986, with college students demonstrating in Halloween masks cheering outside the prison. A similar incident happened in 1970, when a five-year-old Detroit boy named Kevin Toston died of a heroin overdose and heroin was found dusting the wrappers of his Halloween candy; however, it transpired that he had died accidentally after getting into his uncle's stash and the parents had tried desperately to cover it up.

Even if there is no legitimacy to the paranoia around poisoned Halloween candy, these tragic incidents demonstrate that the idea must have been in widespread circulation in the 1970s – widespread enough that the real guilty parties tried to pin their crimes on nebulous figures of abstract malice who are thought to be distributing tainted candy.

And if the relation of this scare lore to *Halloween* seems minor, its lesser, more verifiable cousin, the razor blade in candy, turns up in *Halloween II*. The question presents itself: if this is a holiday about children and fear, are we meant to be afraid *of* children (those devilish pranksters!) or *for* children (the innocent victims of mad poisoners)?

The answer, in the film *Halloween*, is both. Children can kill, and it seems that they can especially kill on October 31st. Even if we cannot know why Michael kills Judith, the fact remains it happens on Halloween night. Children are allowed to adopt a little perversity on Halloween, and are encouraged to play with different personas from behind masks and costumes, and in *Halloween*, the symbolic murder from *Meet Me in St. Louis* becomes real. Elsewhere in *Halloween*, Lonnie Elamb and the other bullies who taunt Tommy with 'The boogeyman's coming!' do not even bother with costumes when they go legend tripping at the Myers house before getting a taste of their own medicine from Loomis. And even after having being terrified by sightings of Michael, Tommy still tries his hand at scaring Lindsay (Kyle Richards) by putting on a scary voice and hiding behind a drape, and later tries to unnerve Lindsay by saying 'He's gonna get you!' during their impromptu pumpkin parade, earning a rebuke from Laurie. Even an awfully nice kid like Tommy has the seeds of perversity in him belying the surface of childhood innocence. Though Laurie's first priority throughout the film's climax is to protect the children, one wonders if they are actually in danger since Michael never attacks them.

The dichotomy of children as victims and children as villains echoes an article authored by the famed anthropologist Margaret Mead for *Redbook* just a few years before *Halloween*, entitled 'Halloween: Where Has All The Mischief Gone?' She recalls fondly her childhood Halloweens spent banging sacks of glass against walls, scrawling impolite words in soap on glass doors and shooting upstairs windows with slingshots.[43] But, she writes, 'that was a far safer world, a world in which adults still believed in adolescent mischief and adolescents believed that mischief had its limits. Mild destructiveness was displaced quite long ago by angry destructiveness and carried out by alienated youngsters against anonymous adults' (1975: 33). Even as Mead understands the reasons for the defanged Halloween that faces her in 1975, she laments:

> Traditionally this was the night where graves yawned, ghosts and skeletons walked abroad and witches and hobgoblins were free to play tricks on mortals. In my

childhood, youngsters in their permitted mischief played out the roles of these characters. Today small children wear the scary costumes, but the characters themselves have been rendered harmless, unfrightening or comic in modern children's literature and television fantasies. (1975: 34)

Mead says that in being redirected more clearly at young children, Halloween fails to provide either scares or the hints of transgression to slightly older ones. Parents now face a difficult task in balancing needs for safety on Halloween without stripping the night of all of its value to children. Mead argues that '[the] older forms of mischief' are essentially lost; children can no longer be allowed to roam free at night, and 'there is no way of telling whether the children who come home are one's own or unknown invaders or whether the people inside the homes will take for granted that the mischief is all in fun or will be angry and hostile to all comers' (ibid.). In other words, the social contract that permitted children to play their pranks on Halloween night without fear of serious repercussions no longer exists.

Children are at the centre of the struggle over what Halloween means that runs through *Halloween*. Is it about candy, as Tommy claims? Is it a night for pranks and legend tripping, as Ronnie Elamb and the other boys think? Is it about relaxed sexual mores (Annie and Lynda)? Or is it a time to try on quasi-parental responsibilities (Laurie)? Sheriff Brackett characterises Haddonfield on a Halloween night thus: 'Nothing's going on. Just kids playing pranks, trick or treating, parking, getting high . . .' But his is a false sense of security. How could Haddonfield, of all towns, forget what Halloween means to it? Loomis knows better, intuiting not only that Michael will return to Haddonfield but that he will do it on Halloween. Michael is driven by a need to pursue the carnivalesque and violent aspects of Halloween (all the more perverse for being so closely wedded to children's culture) to their violent extremes.

What's in a Mask?

It is here where the theme of masking becomes critical. Michael commits Judith's murder wearing a Halloween mask, one previously associated with adolescent foreplay, and stealing another mask is one of his first actions on arriving in Haddonfield. Carpenter has described being influenced by Hervey M. Checkley's book *The Mask of Sanity*. Initially published in 1941 with several updates in subsequent decades, it presents Checkley's clinical research with incarcerated psychopaths, and was indeed the work that popularised that term to the general public. Carpenter says of the book:

> The idea behind it [was that] these folks are not like you and me. And he's talking about truly evil people, the evil of murdering, sociopathic evil that we all recognise when we talk about, when we say that evil is real, that's what we're saying, we're talking about sociopathy. And there's a mask of sanity, where they appear to be sane, I hate to use the word 'normal', but sane like you and me even though they're not. They wear this mask to deceive because they do not feel like you and I do. That's the idea. (author interview)

Michael Myers does not fit very well with Checkley's descriptions of psychopaths, who are generally charming people able to conceal their illnesses in polite society: 'one is confronted with a convincing mask of sanity' (1941: 228). If anything, Michael is their inverse. He wears a mask that reveals his true nature more clearly than his actual face ever could. Loomis describes Michael's face as 'pale, blank, emotionless', and the mask only amplifies that impression.[44] Michael's mask is a key design element in *Halloween*. The modified Shatner mask, itself an off-the-rack Halloween mask, somewhat resembles and may have based on the mask worn by Christiane (Edith Scob) in Georges Franju's poetic masterpiece *Eyes Without a Face* (1960). In both cases, the mask is a stark white, emotionless and inexpressive parody of human features.

Another point of reference may be *The Phantom of the Opera*, especially for the unmasking scene at the very end of the film, when Laurie is struggling with Michael and manages to briefly remove his mask. Here again, though, the relationship must be one of inversion. When Christine Daaé rips the Opera Ghost's mask off it reveals something hideous and inhuman beneath. In *Halloween*, however, the face underneath seems normal, unremarkable. Michael releases Laurie and swiftly puts his mask back on, unable, it seems, to inflict violence without it. The moment echoes the opening sequence, when Michael is stopped in his tracks upon being unmasked by his parents, separated, as it were, from his boogeyman-self when he is deprived, not precisely of anonymity, but of affiliation with Halloween.[45]

The mask in Franju's Eyes Without a Face.

After all, it is not just a mask but a Halloween mask. Like the children in Fraser's experiment, Michael's capacity for aggression seems intrinsically linked with the construction of an alternative persona tied to the mythic space of Halloween. Michael emerges, then, as a distinctive sort of Halloween bogey, as dependent on the holiday for his power as the mythological giant Antaeus was dependent on the Earth. Heracles defeated Antaeus by lifting him into the air; Michael's defeat involves unmasking him, and Michael's paralysis on being unmasked suggests that he needs to play his part in Halloween's mythology to complete his horrifying goals. Laurie's statement to Tommy that the boogeyman can only come out on Halloween night bears this out. Lisa Morton considers the release of *Halloween* to be the key moment in 'the adult reclamation of Halloween' (2012: 97) that would ultimately shift the holiday away from children and towards adult-oriented activities like costume parties and drinking.[46] This shift reminds us of the extent to which Halloween continues to be a space caught between childhood, adolescent and adult vectors.

FOOTNOTES

35.   This is indeed an 'if' – some scholars maintain that Halloween's roots are essentially Christian, despite the claims to the contrary by both neo-pagans and fundamentalist Christians. See Davis (2009).

36.   Not always, though: in the maligned *Halloween III*, Dan O'Herlihy pronounces it correctly.

37. Carpenter tells me he has never read this novelisation. He believes that it was written by Dennis Etchison; he is mis-recalling, but understandably so, because Etchison later novelised *Halloween II* and *Halloween III* under the pseudonym Jack Martin, and *The Fog* under his own byline (as well as writing an unused screenplay for a fourth *Halloween* film). Despite the fact that 'Curtis Richards' is regularly identified as Etchison, including (at this writing) on Etchison's own Wikipedia entry, literary agent Richard Curtis (note the appropriate pseudonym) has said that he wrote the book himself (Curtis 2012).

38. It is tempting to see this as a reference to the murder of Timothy O'Bryan in 1974.

39. According to Lisa Morton, 'Pomona had no festival [and] November was the dullest month in the Roman calendar, with no important holidays or festivals' (2012: 18).

40. This somewhat ignores the fact that, prior to the rise of mischief and hooliganism in the twentieth century, Halloween was a fairly sedate holiday, more associated with romance than horror and violence. We can see this in the Robert Burns poem 'Hallowe'en,' written in 1785.

41. See sociologist Gregory P. Stone's 1959 essay on Halloween, lamenting the fact that costumes, once meant to conceal the identity of young pranksters, were now decorations, and 'trick or treat' was an empty threat.

42. Hence Tommy's description of Halloween as 'when we get candy'. See Honeyman (2008) for more on the association of Halloween and sweets.

43. Note in *Halloween* that Annie's boyfriend Paul (voiced by John Carpenter himself) was grounded for 'throwing eggs and soaping windows', apparently a prank he was pulled *before* Halloween night!

44. However unintentionally, the extended version of *Halloween* underscores that point, since the child actor who plays Michael in the sanitarium does not quite fulfill Loomis's description. For a thorough reading of Michael's masks through a psychoanalytic lens, see Huddleston (2005). She places an emphasis on the mask as a symbol of masculine sexuality.

45. One wonders if a version of Michael with the capacity to speak would howl 'My face!' on being unmasked, the same way Rorschach does in Alan Moore's graphic novel *Watchmen* (1986).

46. This corresponds with Mathijs's point that only after 1978 did it become routine for film studios to release horror films at Halloween (2011: n.p.).

CHAPTER 4: PARENTHOOD, ADOLESCENCE AND CHILDHOOD UNDER THE KNIFE

The fact that the *Halloween* was made by relatively young film-makers may explain how overall youth friendly it is. Speaking of the ill-fated Annie and Lynda, Danny Peary opines: 'Compare the teenage girls in Brian De Palma's *Carrie* (1976) with those in *Halloween* and you'll discover that De Palma still bears hostility toward teenage girls from his adolescence while Carpenter likes them despite their idiosyncrasies' (1991: 125). While I am not sure if is fair to attribute this motivation to De Palma, the point stands that *Halloween*'s girls are drawn with a good deal more detail and affection. This is particularly evident when one compares P.J. Soles's characters in each film, a classic mean girl in *Carrie* and a fun and lovable, if somewhat annoying, party girl in *Halloween* (ample credit must go to Soles for making Lynda's affectation of saying 'totally' in nearly every line more endearing than grating). Tom Allen's review in *The Village Voice* even compared *Halloween* positively to the contemporary teen movie: 'The trio of teenage girls in *Halloween* are victims truly worth caring about. They speak more intelligent dialogue and are more attractively contemporary than the hundreds of blithering idiots in all the Universal, Columbia, and Paramount youth films this year' (1978: 67).

So what does it mean to be 'contemporary' when we are speaking of *Halloween*'s teenagers? Writes Grace Palladino,

> In a sense, teenagers in the 1970s had won the battle for freedom that high school students had been waging since the 1930s. They not only gained a voice and vote in their own affairs, at home and at school, but they had the right to live life as they pleased. Whether adults approved or not, they had to accept the fact that teenagers—girls included—were likely to drink in high school. They had to face up to the unpleasant fact that high school students needed access to reliable birth control, whether parents were willing to discuss the subject or not. Finally, adults had to concede that teenagers lived by their own social rules, rules that had nothing to do with old-fashioned notions of middle-class propriety or respect for the elders. (1996: 244)

And yet, the teenagers did not earn these victories for themselves, but had them bestowed upon them by their forerunners. As such, there was sense that they did not appreciate them and took their privileges for granted. This sense of unearned license marks a crisis in adolescence's parameters and its purpose. Laurie and her friends belong to the 'Lost Generation' later tagged as Generation X by Douglas Coupland, when a breakdown in traditional roles across generations 'paints a picture ... of missing parents, of isolated youth left to raise themselves, and of an adolescence lost without a future' (Brickman, 2012: 21).

Dr. Loomis and Sherriff Brackett meet, oblivious to Michael's presence in the background.

Assessments of *Halloween* as a conservative, reactionary text often rest on the understanding that the permissive culture of the 1970s has resulted in a generation of privileged teenagers in need of being 'scared straight', with Michael Myers 'function[ing] as the punitive bogeyman that stands in for the disciplining parental figure' (Phillips, 2005: 138). Likewise, Tony Williams characterises Michael as 'the return of a patriarchy violently punishing the younger generation' (1996: 211). I have a hard time seeing Michael as a figure of patriarchy in any uncomplicated way, in part because he is so heavily allied with childhood, and in part because he does so much to expose the weaknesses of patriarchy and patriarchal figures. There is no better example of this than when Loomis and Sheriff Brackett meet for the first time on the street, and Michael's stolen car passes behind the police chief and the psychiatrist without either of them noticing. My treatment here sees adolescence as a central theme in *Halloween* in a slightly different way, as invoking (and attempting to resolve) the rootlessness of adolescence in the Lost Generation. Laurie is divided between the realms of adults and children, but this capacity for category mobility ultimately proves valuable. '[C]ast in the roles both of virgin and mother' (Neale, 1981: 25), her ability to properly navigate embrace adult responsibilities and retrain a child's intuition is ultimately what allows Laurie to save herself.

I WAS A TEENAGE PROTAGONIST

The 1950s and John Carpenter's childhood saw the birth of the teen horror film, which followed swiftly on the heels of the 'invention' of the American teenager as a discrete segment of the population, a product of postwar prosperity. Films like *I Was a Teenage Werewolf* (1957), *The Blob* (1958) and *The Giant Gila Monster* (1959) targeted the nascent teenage market as surely as *Rebel Without a Cause* (1955) and *Blackboard Jungle* (1955).[47] In a sense *Halloween* is an inheritor to the 'horror teenpics' or the 'weirdies' of the '50s, and similarly owed much of its success to its ability to knowingly target the large teenage demographic. The slasher films that followed *Halloween* would do the same, and it seems no major exaggeration to say that, if slasher films collectively are 'about' *anything*, they are about adolescence. Their protagonists are almost invariably adolescent and the films resonate with a set of issues about the cultural meanings of adolescence, parenthood and childhood, even as they depend on the disposability of their adolescent characters. In a famous sequence in *Scream*, Randy (Jamie Kennedy) pauses a video of *Halloween* to deliver a frantic lecture on the 'certain rules you must abide by in order to successfully survive a horror movie' to a room full of partying teenagers. The rules are:

1. You can never have sex.

2. You can never drink or do drugs.

3. You should never say 'I'll be right back'.

Of course, if these rules apply at all, they apply to the slasher film in particular rather than to the horror film more broadly, and even then they are a little too rigid; I have often wondered how 'you can't do drugs' can possibly be a rule when the characters in *Scream* are watching *Halloween*, and have presumably just seen Laurie smoking marijuana.

Randy characterises rules 1 and 2 as 'the sin factor', underscoring the general understanding that slasher films are intensely moralistic, almost puritanical, documents. I wonder, however, if we can read them as being less about sin than about maturity. Having sex, drinking, doing drugs – these are all things adolescents in North American culture typically latch on to as gateway activities to adulthood. Laurie's supposed 'purity' is easily exaggerated: she smokes pot, she does not moralise about her friends' clandestine sex lives (and even enables them), and she obviously wants relationships with boys. Even if she is nervous about sex and relationships, she clearly desires them; she is simply a 'late bloomer' in comparison to Annie and Lynda. Her status as the Final Girl has as much to do with her position between childhood and adulthood, mixing a child's intuitive attentiveness to the supernatural and an adult's rationality and capability. Laurie's self-description as 'the old Girl Scout' speaks to this paradox succinctly, melding as it does 'old' and 'girl'. Ironically enough, she says the line after she agrees to take Lindsay off of Annie's hands for the night and allow her rendezvous with boyfriend Paul; the Girl Scouts' value of sisterhood becoming Laurie abetting her friend's irresponsible shirking of her own babysitting duties.

Parents, by and large, are a conspicuous non-presence in *Halloween*. The opening sequence ends with the parents of Michael and Judith unmasking him, stunned and uncomprehending, as the camera pulls back to frame the three of them in a classic triangular composition. It dares us to ask: what kind of parents would raise a tiny murderer? Are they the ones to blame? It is one of the film's mysteries. The film provides no biographical details for the Myers'. They appear to be unremarkable middle class WASPS, and the fact that horror has arisen from their world seems shockingly inexplicable. And yet we are told that this is not a unique and unprecedented case: as the cemetery caretaker says, 'every town has something like this happen'. To prove his point, he relates the story of a man in another town who unexpectedly killed his family with a hacksaw.

Where else are parents in *Halloween*? We fleetingly see Laurie Strode's father onscreen just after the 1978 action moves to Haddonfield. We need the credits to tell us that his name is Morgan Strode (Peter Griffith). He is a realtor, and the sum total of his interactions with his daughter consists of him reminding her to leave a set of keys under the mat at the old Myers place. Though he has less than a minute of screen time, he can be said to trigger the principal events of the film, since this is when Michael first sees

Laurie and begins his stalking of her. Two other sets of parents are nearly completely absent: the Doyles, who have hired Laurie as their babysitter and whom we see fleetingly as the leave the house, and the Wallaces, who have hired Annie.[48]

The only literal parent who figures prominently in *Halloween* is Sheriff Brackett, Annie's father. He is introduced bumping into Laurie on the street and gets one of the film's most ironic lines: 'It's Halloween. I guess everyone's entitled to one good scare.' If the only onscreen interaction between this father and daughter is longer than that between Laurie and Morgan Strode, it is still only one brief scene, a bit of charming banter as the girls stop by the site of a break-in. We wonder if he does not smell the marijuana on his daughter and her friend, or if he is turning a wilful blind eye. Throughout the rest of the film, he appears in his formal capacity as sheriff, a patriarchal figure for the entire town, but if Brackett's task is to protect the children of the town, he fails; nothing the police do throughout *Halloween* comes even remotely close to finding Michael, much less stopping him. The brand of patriarchy on display through Brackett appears benign yet ultimately ineffective. His own daughter dies, but he never learns of it.

When I asked Carpenter why it was necessary to so conspicuously marginalise parents in *Halloween*, he told me:

> I mean it's just the reality of growing up as a kid, you know a lot of what you do is to avoid adult scrutiny. Because you do have your own world ... You're not an adult yet, you don't have to be an adult for a while and you want to have fun and adults, always, always their main job in life is to squelch fun, you know, end the fun. But that's accurate. (author interview)

Carpenter emphasises the separate spheres of the adolescent and the adult, and we can see how neatly those lines are divided in *Halloween*, only colliding in the final scene when Laurie, Dr. Loomis and Michael, the film's three key characters (adolescent, adult and arrested child), finally all come together.

Babysitters, Terrorised and Triumphant

In this near-absence of real parents, the film emphasises surrogate parents. One is, of course, Loomis, a surrogate father to Michael at least and arguably to Laurie as well, and

I will discuss Loomis's narrative role in the next chapter. If Loomis is the film's key figure of patriarchal authority, he, like Brackett, is a failed patriarch, unable to assert his authority over his 'son' and only achieving a partial victory. The parent-surrogates who figure most centrally in *Halloween* are babysitters. As discussed earlier, film was originally conceived under the title *The Babysitter Murders*, and three of the four young women central to the narrative are babysitters. Irwin Yablans conceived the project around the universal accessibility of the idea of babysitting, and Moustapha Akkad explains that this is why he came onto the project: 'The word babysitter clicked with me, because every kid in America knows what a babysitter is' (*Halloween Unmasked*).[49]

Indeed, but what is a babysitter? Miriam Forman-Brunell explores the complex cultural role played by the babysitter, 'the newest profession':

> Represented as villains who have caused danger, and as victims who have courted it, in innumerable stories adults have been telling for almost a century, babysitters have ostensibly damaged property, ruined marriages, and destroyed families . . . The omnipresent babysitter has been notorious for sneaking her boyfriend in the back door, talking on the telephone, sitting glued to the TV, eating her employers out of house and home, and neglecting the children while playing too much attention to the man of the house. This deceptively simple stereotype of the unruly babysitter expresses the anxieties of parents as well as the concern of the culture about teenage girls. (2009: 2)

Much of what Forman-Brunell says here applies to *Halloween*, though none of the girls are home wreckers. Let us bracket for a moment the fact that Judith Myers was Michael's sister: she was also his babysitter, and at that job she was spectacular failure. One irony that becomes evident on repeated viewings of the opening shot is that, where at first we seem to be seeing through the eyes of an outsider penetrating the house, in fact Michael is a six-year-old who never should have been outside of the house on his own at night in the first place. Judith is barely keeping tabs on her charge – 'Michael's around someplace' – and irresponsibly engages in sexual behaviour with her boyfriend. She fits well with the 'unruly babysitter' stereotype, and it seems possible to argue that her brutal punishment by Michael is as much about her neglecting her babysitting responsibilities as her sexual behaviour.

As noted in the introduction, *Halloween* has conceptual links with the urban legend called 'The Babysitter and the Man Upstairs,' in which a teenage girl is terrorised by recurring phone calls while babysitting. Again and again she is asked, 'Have you checked the children?' The girl gets the police to trace the call only to discover that it's coming from inside the house. Depending on the telling, the girl is then confronted by the requisite psycho-on-the-loose and either escapes or dies alongside the children she fails to protect. The legend, first collected in the 1960s, is one of a cluster of tales about inadequate babysitters, like the drug-addled one who accidentally cooks the baby instead of a pot roast. Collectively, the legends speak to fears about girls' shifting roles:

> Though phrased as a rhetorical question, 'Have you checked the children?' was a directive that commanded compliance in females who had grown more cocky... Unable to achieve the sitter's acceptance of the traditional gender system, the maniac's extreme coercion served as a warning to girls that the individual pursuit of desire was detrimental to the safety of domesticity. (Forman-Brunell, 2001: 133–4)

The urban legend warps the role that the telephone stereotypically played in the culture of middle class teenage girls, and so does *Halloween*.[50] Laurie and her friends keep in regular contact though the phone, and Annie, almost the same kind of 'unruly babysitter' as Judith, spends a lot of her time babysitting Lindsay on the phone with either Laurie or Paul. Perverting this 'babysitter network' of communication, Lynda is choked to death by Michael while on the phone with Laurie, who mistakes the call for a prank; the perverse irony of the situation suggests an urban legend in itself. Perhaps the sequence most clearly drawn from 'The Babysitter and the Man Upstairs' is Laurie's trip to the upstairs of the Wallace house, where she sees Michael's grisly handiwork and is attacked by him. The pilfered headstone of Judith Myers sits overtop of the body of Annie, splayed out on the master bed where Lynda and Bob had furtive sex earlier. This is a detail that has long puzzled me; if Michael intends Laurie as his final victim, should not the bed be empty in anticipation of her? Or, one might ask, should not the corpse displayed on the bed be Lynda's, since her post-coital murder more closely mirrors that of Judith? The strongest link between Annie and Judith is that they were both (poor) babysitters. Annie plunks her young charge Lindsey in front of the TV and spends much of her time on the phone, scheming to meet with Paul, ultimately facilitating this goal by depositing Lindsey with Laurie (and not appearing to offer her any share of her babysitting earnings for her trouble!). Michael kills her before she can reach Paul. To say the least, Annie is not very serious about her babysitting: as Lynda says earlier in the film, she only babysits so she has 'a place to …' – Lynda is interrupted before she can fill in 'fuck'. While she is certainly not the home wrecker of the exploitation classic *The Babysitter* (1969), Annie's version of babysitting is similarly wedded to her desire for illicit sex.

Laurie, in contrast, not only does all of her duties to the letter but goes far beyond them. She rises capably against danger, not thinking twice before putting herself in harm's way to protect the children. Whatever the Doyles are paying Laurie, she deserves more! She has an easygoing, affectionate yet firm manner with Tommy (compare the indifferent attitude Annie takes with Lindsay). He even makes her his confidant, showing her the stash of comic books that his mother does not like him to have, yet she is still easily able to adopt a role of authority when he needs sanctioning (tellingly, Tommy sees Laurie as something between a peer and a parent). As much as her quasi-maternal qualities surely mark Laurie as a patriarchal woman, they also ally her with the capable Howard Hawksian woman so beloved of Carpenter. Even when it comes to fighting Michael directly, she keeps her head cool and improvises weapons out of everyday objects, like a knitting needle and a coat hanger. That being said, Laurie is far less of a model Hawksian woman than other Carpenter protagonists (especially Leigh [Laurie Zimmer] in *Assault on Precinct 13*, Melanie Ballard [Natasha Henstridge] in *Ghosts of Mars* [2001] and the characters played by Adrienne Barbeau in *The Fog* and *Escape from New York* [1981]), and the tough-talking, sexually-assertive aspects of the character type actually seem more resident in Annie than Laurie. Laurie's final descent into a traumatised mess, her repeated and frustrating habit of throwing Michael's knife away, and her ultimate need to be rescued by a male figure, Loomis, mark the limits of her self-sustained capability. Likewise, the best-case scenario for the babysitter of the urban legend is to escape alive and let the police handle the madman.

Let us reflect that the only two characters in the film who seem to require no convincing of Michael Myers's danger are Loomis and Tommy Doyle – perhaps the film's premier adult and its premier child. If we accept that Michael is indeed 'the boogeyman', Tommy recognises this before anyone else in Haddonfield. Laurie calms him by enacting a parental role and telling him that the other school kids were just trying to scare him by taunting him about the boogeyman. This is in spite of the fact that she herself has seen some of the same clues about Michael's presence, to which Annie and Lynda, more fully estranged from their own child-selves are fatally oblivious. There is surely a Michael—Tommy nexus at work in *Halloween* as well. Tommy is roughly the same age as Michael was at the time of his crime. Michael spends a protracted sequence watching Tommy from his stolen car, and since Michael is never shown as a threat to children, it seems possible to conclude that he is identifying with him instead.

It is also tempting to identify Michael as an overgrown, arrested child, perhaps not even aware of the consequences of his action ('This isn't a man', as Loomis declares in a different context). Writes Danny Peary, 'There is still a little boy inside a man's body, and everything he does is part of a game' (1991: 126). Peary is surely onto something here; the playful manner in which Michael executes his crimes suggests something quite unlike the moralising avenging angel some take him for. The most obvious case is when he wears a sheet while pretending to be Bob before murdering Lynda. Note too that on two occasions—burglarising a hardware store and stealing Judith's gravestone—Michael's crimes are misattributed to 'kids' by adult authority figures. Robin Wood notes that 'When we have worked our way through all the other liberation movements, we may discover that children are the most oppressed section of the population' (1979a: 10), and one gets a sense of that here, especially since even Laurie initially pays no heed to Tommy's insights about the boogeyman, ultimately borne out as correct. Indeed, it encourages its audience to embrace Tommy's (and ultimately Laurie's) way of seeing the world: the boogeyman, after all, *is real*, and there could well be a monster lurking in every shadow.

In his 1980 interview with Todd McCarthy, Carpenter interestingly describes Laurie as being 'aware of [Michael] because she's more like the killer, she has problems. She's a little uptight, a little bit rigid. She and the killer have a certain link: sexual repression. She's lonely, doesn't have a boyfriend, so she's looking around. And she finds someone—him' (1980: 24).[51] If once again we shift this issue away from sex alone and towards adulthood, then we can understand that Lynda and Annie die not strictly because they have sex (though that unpleasant implication cannot be entirely excised), but because they have cut themselves off too fully from childhood and thus lack Laurie's intuition. The shared repression of Michael and Laurie is complicated by a certain asymmetry: where Michael is the arrested child, Laurie is an intermediary between childhood and adulthood, capable of taking the best from both phases of life. The climax requires her to simultaneously pay heed to the instinctive dread she is feeling, linked so often to childhood and the Halloween rituals of early childhood (again: 'I thought you outgrew superstitions'), and to draw upon an adult's courage and capability as she combats Michael Myers. But of course her self-reliance falters and Loomis steps in to save her. Their only exchange is about as long as Laurie's exchange with her actual father:

Laurie: Was it the boogeyman?
Loomis: As a matter of fact, it was.

The exchange confirms that despite Laurie's dismissals of Tommy's childhood intuition and her own, Tommy was right, and Michael is the materialisation of childhood fears. Of course, the fact that she needs this reassurance from Loomis speaks to the continuing role of patriarchal authority. But this in turn is swiftly undermined by Loomis's inability to capture his quarry, his own symbolic son.

Halloween resonates with then (and still) contemporary fears that adolescents enjoyed adult privileges without adult responsibilities. It gives us a heroine who is defined in large part by being diligent, attentive and responsible, who is invested in the adult world of learning but who has not fully estranged herself from the child within. Laurie has the best of both worlds, and it is through her that the problems of the 'Lost Generation' seem potentially resolvable. This construction of adolescence represents one of *Halloween*'s most optimistic dimensions. And in spite of that, Laurie is not an idealised, 'too-good-to-be-true' youth (an adult's conception of an ideal youth, that is), but is a credible teenager. Much credit must go to Jamie Lee Curtis's warm and natural performance, which skilfully conveys both Laurie's uncertainty and her strength.

But this optimism is undercut by the film's finale. The last we see of her, Laurie is a weeping wreck on the floor of the Doyle house, and I am always left troubled. This is not necessarily because she fails to live up to the standards of later Final Girls, who generally dispatch the slasher personally, but simply because, having spent so much of the film with this bright, engaging character, it is odd and unsatisfying to leave her in this traumatised, damaged, even regressive state. Laurie's ability to tap into her intuitive, childlike dimension and combat Michael is presented positively, but ultimately she becomes a child, unable to save herself without adult help, left looking small and helpless. Her infantilisation is reminiscent of the horrifying final state of Grace Collier (Jennifer Salt) in De Palma's

Sisters, though that film opens itself to a reading emphasising the subjugation of women by patriarchy more readily than *Halloween*; Robin Wood regards *Sisters* as 'the only really radical Feminist film Hollywood has given us since the heyday of Dietrich and Sternberg' (1979b: 63).

Possibly Laurie's condition at the end of the film is meant to mirror that of the audience: terrorised, defeated and lucky to have survived, but I confess that the way the ending leaves Laurie always dismays me (and *Halloween II* continues to show the character little respect, reducing her to catatonia and narrative near-inconsequentiality). It would have made a difference even to let her stand and perhaps join Loomis on the balcony, to end with her head held high rather than weeping on the floor. Even setting aside the obvious gendering of Laurie's final sad state (it is hard to imagine a male protagonist left in a similar position), it undermines the optimistic portrait of the American teenager that the film generally draws. It is dramatically unsatisfying at best and misogynist at worst, and does little justice to this remarkable heroine.

FOOTNOTES

47. See Doherty (1988: 142–78).

48. I have often wondered: where are the parents in *Halloween*? In both 1963 and 1978, Halloween fell on a weekday (a Thursday and a Tuesday, respectively), so what are they all out doing? I put to this question to Carpenter and he confessed he had no idea where they are.

49. The identification of *Halloween* with babysitting is so complete that, in *Scream*, Casey Becker (Drew Barrymore) recalls it as 'The one with the guy in the white mask who walks about and stalks babysitters', which is mostly true, though Lynda is not a babysitter.

50. *Halloween* introduces the importance of the telephone in the first scene. As Judith's boyfriend walks away, we hear her shout 'Will you call me tomorrow?' and he replies with an insensitive, 'Sure, whatever'. One is reminded of Jeffrey Sconce's observations about how the communication technology descending from the wireless creates individual isolation at the same time as it facilitates public communication on a new scale (202: 65). Marc Olivier locates *Halloween*, along with *Black Christmas* and *When a Stranger Calls*, as a 'home-alone-with-a-phone' subgenre of the slasher film, anticipated by William Castle's *I Saw What You Did* (1965) (2013: 32).

51. One might go so far as to suggest that Laurie has somehow unwittingly willed Michael back to Haddonfield in a perverse psychic courtship, hence the refrain of 'I wish I had you all alone,

just the two of us ...' which she even repeats at great length in the extended version. One downside of this approach is the uneasy implication that Laurie is vicariously responsible for Michael's crimes (for a similar reading, see Dika, 1990: 51).

CHAPTER 5: A VERY SINISTER DOCTOR AND A COSMIC MONSTER

As we have noted, Dr. Sam Loomis shares the name of John Gavin's character in Psycho. If a structural likeness between the two Loomises exists, it is that they are nominal heroes who are nonetheless unable to accomplish much of anything until each film's end, when they arrive to stop the villain from killing a young woman. It is tempting, however, to situate Loomis in relation to another character in *Psycho*: Dr. Fred Richmond (Simon Oakland), the psychiatrist who steps into the narrative at the tail end to deliver a lengthy explanation of the manias of Norman Bates (Anthony Perkins). At first glance, Loomis very much exists in contrast to this character. Where Richmond's professional expertise is beyond reproach ('If anybody gets any answers, it'll be the psychiatrist,' Sheriff Chambers states before Richmond appears), Loomis is a more of Cassandra figure: a prophet of doom who knows the truth but is tragically unable to convince anyone of it. And where Richmond is preternaturally confidence in his psychiatric explanations, Loomis has apparently abandoned psychiatry where Michael is concerned.

In Raymond Durgnat's excellent dissection of the psychiatrist's explanation in *Psycho*, he notes that Richmond's coldness and smugness stand in contrast with the 'obvious WASP liberal, à la Peck or Fonda, with his nice combination of grey flannel humanism, careful scruples and quiet, crusading or obstinate, liberalism' (2002: 236). Dr. Loomis is even farther removed from benevolent psychiatrist types like Dr. Luther (Lee J. Cobb) in *The Three Faces of Eve* (1957) than Richmond. 'You must think me a very sinister doctor,' he says after showing Sheriff Brackett that he carries a concealed gun and is trigger happy when spooked. Loomis pays his Hippocratic Oath no heed; having long since given up on curing Michael Myers, he now simply wants to stop him, and is willing to kill to accomplish that goal.

In her history of psychiatry on the screen, Sharon Packer describes Loomis as a psychiatrist who 'makes a deliberate choice to bypass professional ethics, and all known moral codes in order to thwart a greater evil … [*Halloween*] offers a provocative commentary on the alleged leniency of the juvenile justice system, the insanity plea, criminal culpability and mental capacity' (2012: 84–5). Perhaps Packer has a point here:

In room where Judith Myers was killed, Loomis tells Sherriff Brackett about his history with Michael.

Loomis has 'told everybody' that Michael was dangerous but 'Nobody listened!', and he offers a curt 'Because that is the law' when Chambers asks why they are taking Michael before the county judge (and the theme of Loomis being undermined by bureaucracy is played up in the extended version). Finally, however, it seems to me that any commentary *Halloween* offers on any of the subjects Packer lists is fairly minor, and the film's tendency is to defer all earthly considerations of psychiatry to more mythological concerns. Packer goes on to ask, 'If a psychiatrist, who is bound by medical ethics, is willing to break the law when the law does not reach far enough, then why shouldn't an ordinary citizen also take the law into his own hands? Is Loomis simply a vigilante, despite his medical degree?' (2012: 87). I have a hard time see Loomis as a vigilante – he phones the police to warn them about Michael on his way to Haddonfield, and his first action on arriving in town is to present himself to the sheriff, with whom he works closely throughout the film. The fact that the star on Brackett's shoulder is in frame all through Loomis's 'Devil's eyes' monologue visually underscores his association with patriarchy and officialdom. The point remains, however, that Loomis's only accomplishments in the film are entirely outside of his training as a psychiatrist, and may even run counter to it. Terms like 'psychopath', 'schizophrenic' and 'neurotic' appear nowhere in *Halloween*, and even 'catatonic' appears only in the extended television cut. Linda Williams describes Loomis as 'throw[ing] up his hands in unscientific despair at the unfathomable disturbance of nature represented by the psychotic murderer who haunts the streets of a small town' (1981: 64), and Peter Hutchings, alluding to the film's scheme of self-reflexivity, suggests that Loomis, 'alone among the psychiatrists and psychoanalysts who show up in horror, realises that he is in a horror film and modifies his beliefs accordingly' (2004: 62).

Carpenter professes to have no animus against psychotherapy, crediting it with helping him overcome depression in his twenties (author interview). He describes a major inspiration for Michael Myers as coming from a mental institution he visited for a class project while attending Western Kentucky University. He describes seeing a boy with a schizophrenic stare, blank eyes that revealed nothing of whatever thoughts might lurked behind them, and later drawing on that image for the important speech that he places in Loomis's mouth:

> I met him fifteen years ago. I was told there was nothing left, no conscience, no reason, no understanding, in even the most rudimentary sense, of life or death or right or wrong. I met this six-year-old child with this blank, pale, emotionless face and the blackest of eyes, the Devil's eyes. I spent eight years trying to reach him and then another seven trying to keep him locked up because I realized what was living behind that boy's eyes was purely and simply ... evil.

It is remarkable that the image of Michael Myers in his cell, staring at the wall for all those decades, appears nowhere in the film[52] except for as related by Loomis; we never even see the interior of Smith's Grove's Sanitarium. Yet the power of Donald Pleasence's delivery is such that this becomes one of the film's most memorable images, created solely by words.

Loomis reminds one of Nietzsche's famous statement that 'if thou gaze too long into an abyss, the abyss will gaze into thee' (2008: 63). His abyss is Michael; there was 'nothing left' when he became Michael's doctor, just a void in a boy's shell, and those black eyes have consumed the good doctor. Some commentators are convinced that Loomis is insane: 'He seems a bit batty after spending fifteen years with Michael, but we realize it probably takes an insane type to want to track down the indestructible Michael. So we're glad he's on our side' (Peary, 1991: 125). A less charitable interpretation would suggest that Loomis's brand of 'treatment' has made Michael far worse, and has actually reified him into a force of evil by diagnosing him as one.[53]

Numerous points of inspiration for *Halloween* have psychological/psychiatric elements: Checkley's *The Mask of Sanity*, Carpenter's experience in the mental institution, *Psycho*. And as Robin Wood observes, the mere fact of Michael's attempt to recreate his childhood crime, which itself carries the overtones of Freud's primal scene, suggests 'at least the *possibility* of a psychoanalytic explanation' (1979a: 26, original emphasis). Yet the film's psychological elements are a critical stumbling block, since the film actively resists any attempt to see Michael in terms of any identifiable human pathology. Carpenter recalls that 'Nick Castle—who plays the killer—asked me when we were starting production, "Do you want me to act like mentally disturbed people act? Do you want me to have my head back and do inappropriate looks at people and at things?" "Not really!" I answered him' (Boulenger, 2001: 99–101). A verisimilitudinous depiction of mental illness was not on Carpenter's agenda; the creation of a cosmic threat beyond rational explanation, psychological or otherwise, was. The fact that *Halloween* puts so little stock in psychoanalytic explanations creates a certain amount of irony when one considers how extensively it has been subjected to psychoanalysis.[54] All of Loomis's therapeutic methods have not allowed him to understand, let alone help, Michael, and the psychiatric establishment around him has done little to recognise and prepare for the threat that he rightly feels Michael represents. Yet Loomis still repeatedly identifies himself as Michael's doctor. [55]

Carpenter tells me that he conceived of Loomis in reaction to what he perceived as a weakness in *Black Christmas*; the banality of the presentation of its figures of authority, especially Lt. Kenneth Fuller (John Saxon). Says Carpenter,

> I thought my criticism of the movie was that, boy, there's no poetry. It cuts to the police station ... I just thought there's just no elegance in this. I think that was my attempt to get a little bit of that in there. I think that's the only thing I could say – 'Wow, can we have a little bit of something delicious coming out of our guy here?' (author interview)

In addition to such characters as Dr. Richmond, Cassandra and (structurally, at least) Lt. Fuller, Loomis also surely owes something to Captain Ahab, a fact recognised both in scholarship (see Telotte, 1987: 199; Williams, 1996: 216) and cinema (in the self-reflexive slasher film pastiche *Behind the Mask: The Rise of Leslie Vernon* [2006], Loomis's character type is dubbed 'an Ahab'). Loomis also provides a link to another tradition of horror fiction, in which doctors and scientists investigate and confront monsters and supernatural phenomena, with Professor Abraham Van Helsing in Bram Stoker's *Dracula* as an archetypical example. Much of Loomis's portentous dialogue could have gone, say, in the mouth of Edward van Sloane's Van Helsing in *Dracula* (1931), or various other obsessive doctors played by Golden Age stalwarts like Lionel Atwill, George Zucco or Onslow Stevens. Donald Pleasence's very presence stands out as odd and exceptional in the world of *Halloween*: the most familiar actor in the film, much older than the rest of the cast, a classically trained stage-veteran whose theatrical style contrasts with the naturalism of most of the performances, and a British actor in the cast full of Americans. Loomis is an old-fashioned character seemingly visiting *Halloween* from an older mode of horror film.

THE COSMIC MICHAEL MYERS

Loomis is also reminiscent of the tormented scholars who prove to be some of the more capable protagonists in H.P. Lovecraft's short stories, perhaps Dr. Henry Armitage from 'The Dunwich Horror', or Dr. Marinus Bicknell Willett in 'The Case of Charles Dexter Ward'. The latter tale even deals with an escapee from a mental institution and a medical doctor who must defeat his former patient; both Armitage and Willett are men of learning who are drawn into huge-scale supernatural events and come out of them with their sanity more intact than the average Lovecraft protagonist. Carpenter's fondness for Lovecraft is well noted; interviewed in the documentary *Lovecraft: Fear of the Unknown* (2008), Carpenter recalls his father reading 'The Rats in the Walls' and 'The Dunwich Horror' to him in his childhood. Carpenter describes the former tale in terms that apply well to *Halloween*: 'It's really creepy stuff. It gets under your skin. I think it's pretty obvious, when you tear down the walls of any kind of civilised person, there's something behind there that's really abominable.'[56]

Lovecraft's works are famously difficult to adapt: as Carpenter himself noted, 'Once you start reading it, you realise it's in his language. He describes things that are indescribable, the indescribable horror. Some of his best stories are just impossible to visualise' (qtd. in Petley, 2007: 43). Carpenter's debt to Lovecraft is most evident in films like *The Fog*,

The Thing, Prince of Darkness (1987) and especially *In the Mouth of Madness* (1994) (see Mitchell, 2001: 134-41; Powell, 2004; Smith, 2006: 124-5), and smaller homages appear throughout his work.[57] It less noted, however, that *Halloween* has its own indebtedness to Lovecraft's signature mode of 'cosmic horror'. True, Michael bears little resemblance to Lovecraft's ancient, horrifying and often multi-tentacled god-monster-demons with barely pronounceable names like Great Cthulhu, Azathoth, Yog-Sothoth, Shub-Niggurath and Nyarlathotep, 'invented by beings whose vocal organs were not like man's' and which '*hence could never be uttered perfectly by human throats*' (original emphasis) (qtd. in Joshi, 1996: 156).[58] And yet the worldview on display in *Halloween* accords with Lovecraft's in important ways. In a 1927 letter to James F. Morton, Lovecraft wrote: 'Now all my tales are based on the fundamental premise that common human laws and interests and emotions have no validity or significance in the vast cosmos-at-large' (qtd. in Oakes, 2000: 32). Reflecting this mindset, his stories generally depict humans struggling pointlessly against an amoral universe, vastly huge, alien and incomprehensible. Lovecraft's own term for this worldview, derived from his own eccentric reading of writers as diverse as H.G. Wells, Albert Einstein and Ernest Haeckel, was 'cosmic indifferentism':

> He set his stories in a mechanistic-materialist universe which is both soulless and without purpose, governed by undirected, unconscious, blind and, and impersonal forces, that take no account of man's fate, his laws or personal concerns … Lovecraft had created a new kind of horror story by shifting the focus of traditional supernatural dread away from … man's fears of the devil, the dead and the beast in himself to a new crushing realisation that he and all mankind, far from occupying the centre of the cosmic stage even on earth, are scarcely important enough or long-enduring enough to occupy the stage's shabbiest corners. (Campbell, 1996: 169)

Indeed, several times Lovecraft's tales tell us that the mankind's continuing existence depends on alien indifference, as in 'The Whisperer in Darkness': 'They could easily conquer the earth, but have not tried so far because they have not needed to. They would rather leave things as they are to save bother' ([2008e: 676).[59]

Though Carpenter's work is probably more dependent on a 'homocentric' worldview than Lovecraft, Lovecraft's mode of cosmic indifferentism gives us a framework for addressing the old question of what motivates Michael, while reconsidering the film within the generic framework of cosmic horror. 'What does Michael Myers want?' becomes a moot question: Lovecraft's monsters do not have conventional motivations precisely because their natures are not comprehensible to the limited confines of the human mind. It is much the same with Michael. John Kenneth Muir observes that, in *Halloween*, 'people exist pretty much as they did in the caves of our history. Science, medicine, and psychology, the technological and sociological tools man utilises today to rationalise and explain scary or vexing elements of life, are useless in the film' (2000: 76).

One of Lovecraft's more didactic tales is 'The Unnamable', first published in 1925. It contains a debate between Carter, a writer of weird fiction who is one of Lovecraft's numerous semi-autobiographical narrators, and a high school principal named Joel Manton. The two debate whether or not there can exist a being who is not just unnamed but unnamable. Carter believes that there can be: 'And since spirit, in order to cause all the manifestations attributed to it, cannot be limited by any of the laws of matter; why is it extravagant to imagine psychically living dead things in shapes – or absences of shapes – which must for human spectators be utterly and appallingly "unnamable"?' (2008d: 257). By the end of the story, Manton has a supernatural encounter with a being haunting the attic of a nearby house that leads him to agree with Carter that some things are, indeed, intrinsically impossible to name.

Attempts at creating categories and confining everything to the limits of human reason and human language are, for Lovecraft, fraught with folly. The idea of the unnamable monster, existing so far apart from human rationality that it escapes conventional linguistic signification, stands in stark contrast to another tradition of horror that many children become acquainted with through the Rumpelstiltskin narrative. Here the monster not only has a name but can be overcome through an airing of that name. Sometimes this is literally the case, as with the demon Betelgeuse (Michael Keaton) in Tim Burton's *Beetlejuice* (1988) or Superman's impish foe, Mr. Mxyzptlk. But more often, a 'naming' of a more conceptual sort is necessary to defeat a monster: the elaborate set of rules one needs to know to fight a vampire or werewolf, for instance, or the rites of completion needed to banish an uneasy ghost. Such 'naming' narratives are heavily invested in human rationalism, as some of sort of detective work is often needed to yield this valuable, occulted knowledge.

The fact that this is not the case in *Halloween* speaks to its lineage in Lovecraft's world of grim pessimism.[60] It presents a monster that appears to exist entirely apart from real signification of any sort. Michael Myers surely has a name, but that name is banal and inadequate, failing to characterise him in any meaningful way. Addressing Chambers, Loomis does not even refer to him as 'he', but 'it' – stripping away Michael's personhood. Loomis never actually speaks Michael's name at any point in the film, but hardly anyone else does either.[61] His first name is spoken three times in the opening sequence, twice by his sister and once by his father, but never in the 1978-set portion of the film is the name 'Michael' said at all. Even more amazingly, the words 'Michael Myers' are never spoken *anywhere*; 'Myers' is only uttered in relation to Judith Myers and the Myers house. Michael too, it seems, is an unnamable being who resists linguistic signification. He is called by a host of other names: 'Death', 'the Devil', 'purely and simply evil', and, of course, 'the Boogeyman'. All of these are labels of nebulous menace that, importantly, provide the characters with little useful information, but coalesce to reinforce the idea of Michael as an implacable and inexplicable foe, the jest of a cruel cosmos.

Fascinatingly, Michael has another name, too, one that appears only in the closing credits: 'The Shape.' Indeed, 'the Shape' and 'Michael Myers' are even credited separately: Nick Castle as the Shape and Tony Moran as Michael Myers (age 23) and Will Sandin as Michael Myers (age 6).[62] Moran plays Michael when he is unmasked, an important moment in the film to which we will return. When I asked Carpenter why it was necessary to distinguish Michael from the Shape, he said:

> I wanted to suggest that it was something I wanted to do visually. In a lot of scenes he's not really presence necessarily he's just a shape in the distance behind people. And I don't know, it just came to me. And I think the idea in *Halloween* was to, we're saying in the movie that Michael Myers is in fact a human being but I wanted to bleach humanity out of him. I wanted him to be nothing, just like a vessel onto which we could project things. And I think that probably my thinking was call him 'the Shape' and he's just 'The Shape', he's a human shape and he's an absence of humanity, and an absence of anything that smacks of human. (author interview)

Even if Carpenter was not specifically influenced by Lovecraft on this point, Lovecraft often used words like 'shape' in similar ways, to describe something vague, inhuman and inexplicable. Indeed, the closing lines of 'The Unnamable' have Manton crying: 'It was everywhere—a gelatin—a slime—yet it had shapes, a thousand shapes of horror beyond all memory. There were eyes—and a blemish. It was the pit—the maelstrom— the ultimate abomination. Carter, *it was the unnamable!*' (2008d: 261). In 'The Call of Cthulhu', the raving sculptor Castro relates that the Great Old Ones 'were not composed altogether of flesh and blood. They had shape—for did not this star-fashioned image prove it?—but that shape was not made of matter' 2008a: 367). In one of the few excerpts Lovecraft ever provided from the *Necronomicon*, the grimoire written by the fictional Mad Arab Abdul Alhazred, the Old Ones are described as 'differing in likeness from man's truest eidolon to that shape without sight or substance which is Them' ('The Dunwich Horror' 2008c: 645). The word serves Lovecraft in a similar way to its utility to Carpenter: to describe something that is obviously inhuman but is also defined by a lack of clear definition. It is also interesting to note that one place the word 'shape' is heard in *Halloween* is in a line of dialogue from *The Thing from Another World*, which Lindsay is watching: 'C'mon, everybody, we're gonna try to figure out the shape of this thing!' It is followed by the iconic image of the researchers spreading out to discover the shape of a flying saucer frozen into the ice, which Carpenter would affectionately recreate in his remake a few years after *Halloween*. Here again, the word 'shape' is associated with alienness, Otherness and 'thing-ness'.[63]

Lindsay watches The Thing from Another World (1951).

Another concept central to Lovecraft's work also strongly relates to Michael Myers: fate. In the classroom scene, the droning, unseen teacher compares the works of two

authors, Samuels and Costaine, discussing the theme of fate.[64] As Laurie catches her
first glimpse of Michael, standing beside the car across the street staring at her, the
teacher states that, 'In Samuels' writing fate is immovable, like a mountain. It stands
where man passes away. Fate never changes'. Lovecraft's materialistic worldwide is also
grimly fatalistic, in part because his tales generally deal with humans treading into the
world of beings so advanced that their agency is utterly inadequate, and indeed humans
are closer on the cosmic scale to amoebas. Characters struggle against fate but rarely
prevail, and sometimes the fates of cities or worlds are sealed, no matter what anyone
does. The best outcome in a Lovecraft story is often a mere deferral of the inevitable, as
in 'The Call of Cthulhu', where we know that the reawakening of Great Cthulhu related
in the story was only temporary, or else the entire world would be 'screaming with
fright and frenzy' (2008a: 379). But Cthulhu *will* return eventually; it is fated. The end of
Halloween is likewise fatalistic. At best, Michael Myers has only been handed a setback.

James Campbell describes two opposing Lovecraft character types: 'the initiated
human who knows and goes insane and the knowing human who adjusts to human
insignificance in the cosmos' (1996: 189). Loomis can be seen in terms of the latter type,
or perhaps even as a conflation of the two. 'Your compassion is overwhelming, doctor,'
spits Chambers at Loomis as they approach Smith's Grove early in the film. Compassion,
it seems, has been burned out of Loomis during his years as Michael's doctor. In the
first lines of 'The Call of Cthulhu' the unhinged narrator famously opines that, 'The most
merciful thing in the world, I think, is the inability of the human mind to correlate all its
contents. We live on a placid island of ignorance in the midst of black seas of infinity,
and it was not meant that we should voyage far' (2008a: 355). One can imagine Loomis
saying those very words; perhaps the black seas of infinity reside within Michael Myers'
black eyes. We may think of *Halloween*'s psychological themes, at the centre of which
Loomis stands, in terms of something we often find in gothic and horror fiction: the
conflation of the cosmic and the internal spaces of the mind.[65] Michael is a creature
of darkest recesses of the unconscious *and* a cosmic foe from outside of humanity.
This homology between the world of the supernatural and the unconscious possibly
gets articulated in Loomis's lines from *Halloween II* – 'Samhain isn't the evil spirits, it's
not goblins and ghosts or witches. It's the unconscious mind. We're all afraid of the
dark inside ourselves' – more clearly than anything in *Halloween* itself, but it is to the

first film's credit that it need not be so literal. Loomis, we might say, is a man who has pierced that veil of ignorance and looked at the horrors that lie beyond (or, perhaps, deep within) the human consciousness and returned (semi-) sane to protect the rest of us from the monsters that live there.

And this takes us back to the odd status of Loomis's psychiatry in *Halloween*. In an often ignored aside in his famous essay on the Uncanny, Freud notes that diseases like hysteria and epilepsy were once attributed to supernatural, demonic forces and retain those qualities for many. Psychoanalysis, which is 'concerned with laying bare these hidden forces' (1964: 44), becomes an uncanny science in its own right, the therapist being a new face of the beneficial master who can set the world right through occult powers. So if it seems strange on the diegetic level that Loomis's battle with Michael requires such a forsaking of his professional role, on a meta-narrative level it still feels right: the unconscious (tinged with the cosmic) is a staging ground for the battle of good and evil, and Loomis, therapist slayer of dragons, becomes an implausible fairy tale white knight.

FOOTNOTES

52. Again, excluding the extended cut.
53. Wood also notes that the film flirts with the notion that 'Michael's "evil" is what his analyst has been projecting onto him,' but goes on to say, 'Unfortunately, this remains merely a possibility in the material that Carpenter chose not to take up: it does not constitute a legitimate (let alone a coherent) reading of the actual film' (1979a: 26).
54. For instance, see Huddleston (2005). It should be noted that Carpenter himself has invoked the Oedipus complex as an explanation for Michael's murder of Judith (Boulenger, 2001: 99).
55. We have reason to doubt Loomis's intuition into Michael's behavior, however—Loomis is certain that Michael will return to the Myers house, but he never does.
56. Carpenter also speaks of Lovecraft's influence on his work in Milgoire and Strysik (2006: 36-43).
57. For instance, 'Arkham,' the name of the fictional Massachusetts town where many of Lovecraft's stories take place, is used as a name for a building in *Someone's Watching Me!* and a reef in *The Fog*. Carpenter wrote the screenplay for *They Live* under the pseudonym 'Henry Armitage.'
58. But does not the famous chant from 'The Call of Cthulhu': '*Ph'nglui mglw'nafh Cthulhu R'lyeh wgah'nagl fhtagn*'/'In his house at R'lyeh dead Cthulhu waits dreaming' (2008a: 363) adjust very easily to 'In Smith's Grove Sanitarium Michael Myers waits staring'? As Cumbow notes, 'the

resurgence of an age-old evil, waiting for its time' (2000: 148) is a favourite Carpenter theme.

59. Other sources on the theme of cosmicism in science fiction and horror include Lévy (1988) and Stableford (2007).

60. Lovecraft actually disputed that indifferentism was the same thing as pessimism, and argued that 'Pessimists are just as illogical as optimists; insomuch as both envisage the aims of mankind as unified, and as having a direct relationship … to the inevitable flow of terrestrial motivation and events' (qtd. in Joshi, 1996: 147).

61. I am omitting the extended version, where Loomis does speak the name 'Michael Myers' twice.

62. Whoever wrote these credits should not be praised for their arithmetic skills, apparently thinking that $6 + 15 = 23$.

63. See Botting (2012) for a fascinating treatment of the 'Thing' as a concept in horror and philosophy.

64. These authors are fictional (author interview).

65. And not only fiction: Freud himself maintained a longstanding interest in spiritualism, occultism and psychical research, and some of his disciples, including Sandor Ferenczi and Carl Jung, went farther. Writes Roger Luckhurst, 'Among the bizarraries of "proven" spirits in Victorian psychologies, it seems to me that Freud hovered indecisively at the edges, not simply for reasons of siding with exact Science or the prudential await of positivistic proof that never arrived, but because he sensed something about the ghostly that could add, incalculably, to psychoanalysis' (1996: 65). See also Thurschwell (2001). This curious alliance between psychoanalysis and the supernatural stands in contrast to Todorov's assertion that 'Psychoanalysis has replaced (and thereby made useless) the literature of the fantastic. There is no need to resort to the devil in order to speak of an excessive sexual desire, and none to resort to vampires in order to designate the attraction exerted by corpses: psychoanalysis, and the literature which is directly or indirectly inspired by it, deal with these matters in undisguised terms' (1973: 161).

CONCLUSION: 'PURELY AND SIMPLY EVIL'

In the *Halloween* sequels, the word 'evil' practically becomes Loomis's catchphrase, resulting in such gems of bad dialogue as 'We're not talking about any ordinary prisoner! We're talking about evil on two legs!' (from *Halloween 4: The Return of Michael Myers* [1988]). It is used three times in the first film, all by Loomis: 'The evil is gone,' Loomis says after Michael escapes from Smith's Grove, and later he tells Brackett about realising that 'What was living behind that boy's eyes was purely and simply evil', as well mentioning Michael's incapacity for telling the difference between good and evil. Throughout this book, I have explored ways in which Michael can be seen as much more than a murderous psychopath: a ghost, an urban legend, a Halloween bogey or a cosmic monster. But all of these discussions have skirted this question of Michael as an abstract embodiment of pure evil. What can this mean?

First, an appeal to Christianity does not seem to do much to explain Michael's kind of evil, despite the Loomis's claim that Michael has 'the Devil's eyes'. Michael does not seem to be doing Satan's work. He is not corrupting, just killing. Carpenter says he has never really understood the 'Christian conception of evil [as] personified by Satan, Lucifer, who's an Angel who led a rebellion against God, of all things... and got kicked out and is causing havoc amongst Gods' beloved … but it doesn't make sense because we're supposedly evil, all men are sinners, got the devil in us' (author interview).

In a 2012 interview for dailgrindhouse.com, Carpenter said of Bowling Green, Kentucky, where he was raised: 'I will give the town something, though; everything I learned about evil I learned in that little town.' Asked for clarification, he stated 'In every way you can imagine. The way people treat each other. The way people treat outsiders [which Carpenter and his family were] … this was the Jim Crow era so there was some pretty outrages [sic] things going on'. In an interview with Gilles Boulenger, he described the racial injustices in Bowling Green at much greater length. He talks about how an ex-girlfriend's grandfather once fatally rammed a black man in the street with his car for no other reason than 'he didn't like the way the nigger was walking across the street' (2001: 60) and how he had high school friends who liked to drive around town and shoot at black people. Says Carpenter, 'there is never going to be a part of me that will understand the two friends of mine who went shooting African-Americans on a Saturday night with guns. I'm not trying to be hyperbolical; I just don't understand this. It's totally evil!' (2001: 61).

The acts that Carpenter observed in Bowling Green fall under the heading of what some scholars call 'moral evils': 'they are in some sense the result of someone who is morally blameworthy of the resultant evil. There was an intention behind the event, and a person's free will was involved' (Meister, 2012: 3). These would appear to be acts of evil of a type of which Michael Myers is not capable, since, in Loomis's own assessment, he lacks a sense of right and wrong. Still, it is interesting how Carpenter displaces the evil onto the town of Bowling Green itself, presumably not to absolve the guilt of any individuals involved, but to characterise the overall climate that made these evils thinkable. It corresponds with the characterisation of Haddonfield as a haunted environment.

In place of Hannah Arendt's 'banality of evil' – the horrifying awareness that massive evils like the Holocaust are perpetrated by ordinary people serving an evil system – Carpenter gives us more of an 'anonymity of evil', with evil simultaneously localised within an individual and made faceless, traceless and inexplicable. If *Prince of Darkness* stems from Carpenter '[w]anting to do a movie about rationalized fear, rationalized evil' (Boulenger, 2001: 203), where moral categories of good and evil take on a pseudo-scientific character, *Halloween* does the opposite, constructing a seemingly irrational evil, stripped of personality, of details, of specifics. As Carpenter explains, this blankness was designed to allow the audience to 'project their own feelings and thoughts and fears into this character so he's more than what he was, more than what was there' (author interview).

The film works formally to underscore's Michael's status as a dehumanised and abstract 'evil'. And yet, as we have seen, the film does so much to blur his perspective with that of the camera and the audience, hinting at an evil potential residing in cinema itself. Is *Halloween*, then, an *evil film*? This is not a new concept. In 1915, the U.S. Supreme Court denied free speech protection to cinema based on the medium's '[capacity] for evil, having power for it, the greater because of the attractiveness and manner of exhibition' (qtd. in Gunning, 2004: 22). Tom Gunning locates this judgment within a long tradition in western culture of iconophobic distrust of systems of images: 'cinema's power for evil may lie precisely in its lack of certainty, its maintenance of a realm of illusion rather than clearcut revelation' (2004: 33). *Halloween*, like so many horror films, crafts an uncanny world of illusion and deception and uncertainty, reified in Michael. To a certain way of thinking, *Halloween* is evil in just the way that Supreme Court forecasted.

Possibly we need to shift the issue from moral philosophy to cinematic presentation, from 'evil' to 'villainy'. Rothman draws an opposition between theatrical melodrama with its stark categories of good and evil with cinematic villainy, which (Rothman argues) undermines presentations of 'pure evil' by embedding it too strongly in the human:

> Perfect human representatives of evil are not real; human beings wish for them and theatrical melodrama is motivated in part by that wish. But the camera reveals that human beings are only humans. When they appear inhuman, as they often do in films, the camera (which human beings also wish for) participates in creating that inhumanity. Evil, understood as an occult force that exists apart from human beings and their creations, has no reality in the face of the camera. (2004: 81)

Michael Myers studies the body of Bob.

Indeed, cinematic villains are often designated as pure evil but come off as less evil than intended simply because of the humanising touches performance inevitably adds. Carpenter worked against this tendency through the presentation of Michael Myers, so calculated to exclude everything that is human. Yet some humanising moments sneak into *Halloween* almost of in spite of this strategy. After murdering Bob, pinning him to the wall with a butcher's knife, Michael stands cocking his head from side to side. Is he admiring his handiwork? Or is he puzzled by the reality of death? It reminds me of that great moment in *King Kong* (1933), after Kong finishes killing the tyrannosaur and then takes an idle moment to play with its lifeless jaws, transformed into a playful ape. There is a similar moment shortly afterwards, after Michael kills Lynda and holds the telephone up to his ear. This is one of the few close ups of Michael, and while it can be interpreted as a sinister moment, with Michael listening to Laurie's voice (and hijacking the network of babysitter communication) and identifying his ultimate victim, I find there is something weirdly forlorn about the image. Does Michael even remember how a telephone works?

Michael listens to Laurie's voice over the telephone.

Mostly, however, the mask, which both resembles but is clearly not a human face, works to winnow away the human factor from Michael Myers. Like an actor in a Greek drama, Michael wears his villainy plainly on his face. We return to the unmasking moment at the end of *Halloween*, which John Kenneth Muir refers to as 'strange and timeless' (2000: 79), so pure is the triangulation of character-types in this sequence: villain (Michael), victim (Laurie) and hero (Loomis). Placed in the Arthurian context that would match the story Laurie abortively reads to Tommy, we can rename this triad as 'dragon', 'damsel' and 'white knight'. The last minute rescue would make D.W. Griffith proud. And yet, typical of *Halloween*'s overall self-awareness, it brings a reflexive edge to the familiar scene. The removal of the mask briefly seems to make everyone unsure of their role in the drama.

Michael stops strangling Laurie, giving her enough time to escape, and Loomis does not take his first shot until the mask is safely back in place.

The exchange 'Was it the boogeyman?' 'As a matter of fact, it was,' which I previously discussed as validating a child's way of seeing the world, opens itself up to a different reading: Laurie and Loomis need to reinforce their own parts in the drama of good and evil, to deny any implication that Michael was just a man of flesh and blood. From here, it is only a small stretch to provide an answer for the question of Michael's motivation, which is only a small variation on my proposition in the introduction that we should accept that he has none. Could it be that Michael is simply and purely motivated to be a villain in a horror film? I do not raise this possibility glibly; it seems appropriate to the film's self-reflexive play with cinema and evil.

It is an off-repeated piece of trivia that, filming the final scene of *Halloween*, Donald Pleasence offered to play his reaction to Michael's disappearance two ways, one with surprise and the other with an attitude of 'I expected that to happen', and that Carpenter chose the latter footage in editing. Loomis's face reflects not surprise but confirmation, and this was indeed the right choice for a variety of reasons, including for the film's scheme of self-reflexivity. If Loomis, as Peter Hutchings suggests, 'realises that he is in a horror film' (2004: 62), he ought to know that the monster is never really gone for good. Laurie seems to know this too, for the film cuts to her crying all the more intensely, even though she should have no way of knowing what Loomis is seeing. Since Carpenter and Hill insist that they did not make the film with a sequel in mind, we can interpret its open ending in other ways, including within generic tradition. It was not a sequel hook, since the film-makers had no dreams of the film being successful enough to warrant a sequel: like the words 'The End' converting to a giant question mark at the close of *The Blob*, it is an articulation of the fact that monsters do not go away for long, not so long as all those things they can represent are still with us. The disappearance of Michael and his subsequent dispersal into the ether of Haddonfield deliver a similar point: the monster never really dies, and we are never really safe. We all know this, so why do we ever pretend otherwise?

And indeed, Michael Myers *has* never died, either diegetically or in the public mind. Thanks to Irwin Yablans and Moustapha and Malek Akkad, he has taken on numerous incarnations in the decades since 1978, interpreted by dozens of individual writers and directors. It is even said that it is contractually impossible to kill him (for good, that is)! It is pure speculation to imagine what would have happened if Carpenter had had his way and *Halloween II* never been made; but even if *Halloween* had not proven to be the lynchpin of a long-running movie series and an enormous media empire, I suspect it would still be remembered much as it is today: as a beloved and influential classic horror film, a 'stylistic exercise', yet so much more.

WORKS CITED

Allen, Tom. 'A Sleeper That's Here to Stay.' *The Village Voice*. New York. November 6, 1978, 67–70.

Bannatyne, Lesley Pratt. *Halloween: An American Holiday, an American History*. New York: Pelican, 1998.

Bannatyne, Lesley Pratt. *Halloween Nation: Behind the Scenes of America's Fright Night*. Gretna, LA: Pelican, 2011.

Botting, Fred. 'More Things: Horror, Materialism and Speculative Weirdism.' *Horror Studies* 3.3 (2012): 281–303.

Boulanger, Gilles. *John Carpenter: The Prince of Darkness*. Los Angeles: Silman-James Press, 2001.

Bradbury, Ray. *The Halloween Tree*. New York: Alfred A. Knopf, 1972.

Brickman, Barbara Jane. *New American Teenagers: The Lost Generation of Youth in 1970s Films*. London: Continuum, 2012.

Brophy, Philip. 'Horrality – The Textuality of Contemporary Horror Films.' *The Horror Reader*. Ed. Ken Gelder. London: Routledge, 2000, 276-84.

Brummett, Barry. 'Electric Literature as Equipment for Living: Haunted House Films.' *Critical Studies in Mass Communication* 2 (1985): 246–61.

Brunvand, Jan Harold. *The Vanishing Hitchhiker: American Urban Legends and Their Meanings*. New York: W.W. Norton, 1981.

Burnand, David and Miguel Mera. 'Fast and Cheap? The Film Music of John Carpenter.' *The Cinema of John Carpenter: The Technique of Terror*. Eds. Ian Conrich and David Woods. London: Wallflower Press, 2004, 49-64.

Campbell, James. 'Cosmic Indifferentism in the Fiction of H.P. Lovecraft.' *American Supernatural Fiction: From Edith Wharton to the Weird Tales Writers*. New York: Garland Publishing, 1996, 167-228.

Carpenter, John. Telephone interviews with the author, August 20, 2012 and February 25, 2013.

Carroll, Noël. *The Philosophy of Horror, or Paradoxes of the Heart*. New York: Routledge, 1990.

Checkley, Hervey. *The Mask of Sanity*. St. Louis: The C.V. Mosby Company, 1941.

Chion, Michel. *The Voice in Cinema*. New York: Columbia University Press, 1999.

Christensen, Kyle. 'The Final Girl Versus Wes Craven's *A Nightmare on Elm Street*: Proposing a Stronger Model of Feminism in Slasher Horror Cinema.' *Studies in Popular Culture* 34.1 (Fall 2011): 23–44.

Clover, Carol J. *Men, Women and Chain Saws: Gender in the Modern Horror Film*. Princeton: Princeton University Press, 1992.

Connolly, Kelly. 'Defeating the Male Monster in *Halloween* and *Halloween H20*.' *Journal of Popular Film & Television* 35.1 (Spring 2007): 12–20.

Creed, Barbara. *The Monstrous-Feminine: Film, Feminism, Psychoanalysis*. London: Routledge, 1993.

Cumbow, Robert C. *Order in the Universe: The Films of John Carpenter* (Second Edition). London: Scarecrow, 2000.

Curtis, Richard. 'Writing John Carpenter's 'Halloween' Novelization.' *Publishing in the 21st Century*. October 16, 2012. http://curtisagency.com/blog/2012/10/writing-john-carpenters-halloween.html. Accessed January 6, 2013.

Daily Grindhouse. Interview with John Carpenter. May 1, 2012. http://dailygrindhouse.com/thewire/john-carpenter-the-daily-grindhouse-interview/ Accessed February 10, 2012.

Danielson, Larry. 'Folklore and Film: Some Thoughts on Baughman Z500-599.' *Western Folklore* 38.3 (July 1979): 209–19.

Davis, Robert A. 'Escaping Through Flames: Halloween as a Christian Festival.' *Trick or Treat? Halloween in a Globalising World*. Eds. Malcolm Foley and Hugh O'Donnell. Newcastle upon Tyne: Cambridge Scholars Press, 2009, 28-44.

Dika, Vera. *Games of Terror: Halloween, Friday the 13th, and the Films of the Stalker Cycle*. Rutherford: Associated University Presses, 1990.

Doherty, Thomas. *Teenagers and Teenpics: The Juvenilization of American Movies in the 1950s*. Boston: Unwin, 1988.

Donnelly, K.J. *The Spectre of Sound: Music in Film and Television*. London: BFI, 2005.

Driscoll, Catherine. *Teen Film: A Critical Introduction*. Oxford: Berg, 2011.

Durgnat, Raymond. *A Long, Hard Look at 'Psycho'*. London: BFI, 2002.

Ebert, Roger. *Roger Ebert's Four-Star Reviews 1967-2007*. Kansas City: Andrews McMeel, 2007.

Ellis, Bill. 'Legend Tripping in Ohio.' *Papers in Comparative Studies* 23 (1982/3): 61–73.

Ellroy, James. *American Tabloid: A Novel*. New York: Ivy Books, 1995.

Farber, Manny. 'Val Lewton.' *Negative Space: Manny Farber on the Movies*. New York: Da Capo Press, 1998.

Forman-Brunell, Miriam. *Babysitter: An American History*. New York: New York University Press, 2009.

Freeland, Cynthia A. 'Realist Horror.' *Philosophy and Film*. Eds. Cynthia A. Freeland and Thomas E. Wartenberg. London: Routledge, 1995, 126-42.

Freud, Sigmund. 'The 'Uncanny'.' *The Standard Edition of the Complete Psychological Works of Sigmund Freud. Vol. XVII* (1917-1919). London: Hogarth Press. 1964.

Gentner, Robert. 'Imagining Murderous Mothers: Male Spectatorship and the American Slasher Film.' *Studies in the Humanities* 33.1 (June 2006): 101–23.

Gill, Pat. 'The Monstrous Years: Teens, Slasher Film, and the Family.' *Journal of Film and Video* 52.4 (Winter 2002): 16–30.

Goddu, Teresa A. *Gothic America: Narrative, History and Nation.* New York: Columbia University Press, 1997.

Goldstein, Diane E., Sylvia Ann Grider and Jeannie Banks Thomas. *Haunting Experiences: Ghosts in Contemporary Folklore.* Logan: Utah State University Press, 2007.

Gunning, Tom. 'Flickers: On Cinema's Power for Evil.' *Bad: Infamy, Darkness, Evil and Slime on Screen.* Ed. Murray Pomerance. Albany: SUNY University Press, 2004, 21-38.

Gunning, Tom. 'Uncanny Reflections, Modern Illusion: Sighting the Modern Optical Uncanny.' *Uncanny Modernity: Cultural Theories, Modern Anxieties.* Eds. Jo Collins and John Jervis. Houndmills, Basingstoke, Hants: Palgrave Macmillan, 2008, 68-92.

Halloween: A Cut Above the Rest. Prod. Michele Farinola. *Halloween.* Dir. John Carpenter. Anchor Bay, 2007. Blu-Ray.

Halloween Unmasked. Dir. Mark Cerulli. *Halloween.* Dir. John Carpenter. Anchor Bay, 2000. DVD.

Hardy, Phil. *The Encyclopedia of Horror Movies.* New York: Harper and Row, 1986.

Hills, Matt. *The Pleasures of Horror.* London: Continuum, 2005.

A History of Horror. Dir. John Dass. BBC, October 2010.

Honeyman, Susan. 'Trick of Treat? Halloween Lore, Passive Consumerism, and the Candy Industry.' *The Lion and the Unicorn* 32.1 (2008): 82–108.

Huddleston, Jason. 'Unmasking the Monster: Hiding and Revealing Male Sexuality in John Carpenter's *Halloween.*' *Journal of Visual Literacy* 25.2 (Autumn 2005): 219–36.

Humphries, Reynold. *The American Horror Film: An Introduction.* Edinburgh: University of Edinburgh Press, 2002.

Hutchings, Peter. *The Horror Film.* Harlow, Essex: Pearson Education, 2004.

Jancovich, Mark. "General Introduction." *Horror: The Film Reader.* London: Routledge, 2002. 1-19.

Joshi, S.T. 'H.P. Lovecraft: The Fiction of Materialism.' *American Supernatural Fiction: From Edith Wharton to the Weird Tales Writers.* New York: Garland Publishing, 1996, 141-68.

Kael, Pauline. 'Review of *Halloween.*' *The New Yorker* February 19, 1979: 128.

Kehr, Dave. '*Halloween*.' *When Movies Mattered: Reviews from a Transformative Decade*. Chicago: University of Chicago Press, 2011, 72-4.

Kendrick, Walter. *The Thrill of Fear: 250 Years of Scary Entertainment*. New York: Grove Weiderfeld, 1991.

King, Stephen. *Danse Macabre*. New York: Everest, 1981.

Kinsella, Michael. *Legend-Tripping Online: Supernatural Folklore and the Search for Ong's Hat*. Jackson: University Press of Mississippi, 2011.

Knight, Deborah and George McKnight. '*American Psycho*: Horror, Satire, Aesthetics, and Identification.' *Dark Thoughts: Philosophic Reflections on Cinematic Horror*. Lanham, MD: Scarecrow Press, 2003, 212-229.

Koven, Mikel J. *Film, Folklore and Urban Legends*. Lanham, MD: Scarecrow, 2008.

Leeder, Murray. 'Ghost-Seeing and Detection in Stir of Echoes.' *Clues: A Journal of Detection*. 30.2 (2012): 76-88

Leeder, Murray. 'Skeletons Sail an Etheric Ocean: Approaching the Ghost in John Carpenter's *The Fog*.' *Journal of Popular Film and Television*. 37.2 (2009): 70–9.

Lévy, Maurice. *Lovecraft: A Study in the Fantastic*. Detroit: Wayne State University Press, 1988.

Leydon, Rebecca. '*Forbidden Planet*: Effects and Affects in the Electro Avant-garde.' *Off the Planet: Music, Sound and Science Fiction Cinema*. Ed. Philip Hayward. Eastleigh: John Libbey, 2006. 61–76.

Lovecraft, H.P. 'The Call of Cthulhu.' *H.P. Lovecraft: The Complete Fiction*. New York: Barnes & Noble, 2008a, 355-79.

Lovecraft, H.P. 'The Case of Charles Dexter Ward.' *H.P. Lovecraft: The Complete Fiction*. New York: Barnes & Noble, 2008b, 490-593.

Lovecraft, H.P. 'The Dunwich Horror.' *H.P. Lovecraft: The Complete Fiction*. New York: Barnes & Noble, 2008c, 633-667.

Lovecraft, H.P. 'The Unnamable.' *H.P. Lovecraft: The Complete Fiction*. New York: Barnes & Noble, 2008d, 256-61.

Lovecraft, H.P. 'The Whisperer in Darkness.' *H.P. Lovecraft: The Complete Fiction*. New York: Barnes & Noble, 2008e, 668-722.

Lowenstein, Adam. 'A Reintroduction to the American Horror Film.' *The Wiley-Blackwell History of American Film* V.4. Ed. Cynthia Lucia, Roy Grundmann and Art Simon. Malden, MA: Wiley-Blackwell, 2012. 154-76.

Luckhurst, Roger. "Something Tremendous, Something Elemental" On the Ghostly Origins of Psychoanalysis.' *Ghosts: Deconstruction, Psychoanalysis, History*. Eds. Peter Buse and Andrew Stott. Houndmills, Basingstoke, Hants: Macmillan, 1999, 50-71.

Mathijs, Ernest. 'Threat or Treat: Film, Television, and the Ritual of Halloween.' *FlowTV* 11.01 (2011). http://flowtv.org/2009/10/threat-or-treat-film-television-and-the-ritual-of-halloween-ernest-mathijs-the-university-of-british-columbia/

McCarthy, John. *Splatter Movies: Breaking the Last Taboo of the Screen*. New York: St. Martin's Press, 1984

McCarthy, Todd. Interview with John Carpenter. 'Trick and Treat.' *Film Comment* 16 (1980): 17–24.

Mead, Margaret. 'Halloween: Where Has All The Mischief Gone?' *Redbook* 145 (October 1975), 31–33.

Meister, Chad. *Evil: A Guide for the Perplexed*. London: Continuum, 2012.

Milgiore, Andrew and John Strysik. *The Lurker in the Lobby: A Guide to the Cinema of H.P. Lovecraft*. Seattle: Armitage House, 2000.

Mitchell, Charles P. *The Complete H.P. Lovecraft Filmography*. Westport: Greenwood Press, 2001.

Morton, Lisa. *Trick or Treat: A History of Halloween*. London: Reaktion, 2012.

Muir, John Kenneth. *The Films of John Carpenter*. Jefferson NC: McFarland, 2000.

Neale, Steve. '*Halloween*: Suspense, Aggression and the Look.' *Framework* 14 (1981): 25–29.

Nelson, Andrew Patrick. 'Traumatic Childhood Now Included: Todorov's Fantastic and the Uncanny Slasher Remake.' *American Horror Film: The Genre at the Turn of the New Millennium*. Jackson: University Press of Mississippi, 2010, 140-54.

Newman, Kim. *Nightmare Movies: Horror on Screen since the 1960s*. London: Bloomsbury, 2011.

Nietzsche, Friedrich. *Beyond Good and Evil*. Rockville, MD: Serenity Publishers, 2008.

Nowell, Richard. *Blood Money: A History of the First Teen Slasher Film Cycle*. New York: Continuum, 2011.

Nowell, Richard. '"A Kind of Bacall Quality": Jamie Lee Curtis, Stardom, and Gentrifying Non-Hollywood Horror.' *Merchants of Menace: The Business of Horror Cinema*. New York: Bloomsbury Academic, forthcoming.

Oakes, David A. *Science and Destabilization in the Modern American Gothic: Lovecraft, Matheson, and King*. Westport: Greenwood Press, 2000.

Olivier, Marc. 'Gidget Goes Noir: William Castle and the Teenage Phone Fatale.' *The Journal of Popular Film and Television* 41.2 (2013): 41–52.

Packer, Sharon. *Cinema's Sinister Psychiatrists: From Caligari to Hannibal*. Jefferson, NC: McFarland, 2012.

Palladino, Grace. *Teenagers: An American History*. New York: BasicBooks, 1996.

Paul, William. *Laughing Screaming: Modern Hollywood Horror and Comedy*. New York: Columbia University Press, 1994.

Peary, Danny. *Cult Movies. The Classics, the Sleepers, the Weird and the Wonderful*. New York: Delta, 1991.

Petley, Julian. 'The Unfilmable? H.P. Lovecraft and the Cinema.' *Monstrous Adaptations: Generic and Thematic Mutations in Horror Film*. Manchester: Manchester University Press, 2007, 50-71.

Phillips, Kendall. *Projected Fears: Horror Films and American Culture*. Westport: Praeger, 2005.

Powell, Anna. '"Something Came Leaking Out'': Carpenter's Unholy Abominations.' *The Cinema of John Carpenter: The Technique of Terror.* Eds. Ian Conrich and David Woods. London: Wallflower Press, 2004, 35-47.

R.A. the Rugged Man. 'R.A. interviews Horror Icon JOHN CARPENTER director of HALLOWEEN and THE THING.' *R.A. the Rugged Man.* August 5, 2011. http://ratheruggedman.net/2011/08/760/

Rathgeb, Douglas L. 'Bogeyman from the Id: Nightmare and Reality in *Halloween* and *A Nightmare on Elm Street*.' *Journal of Popular Film & Television* 19.1 (1991): 36–43.

Rogers, Nicolas. *Halloween: From Pagan Ritual to Party Night.* Oxford: Oxford University Press, 2002.

Rosenbaum, Jonathan. '*Halloween*.' *Take One* 7.2 (January 1979): 8–9.

Rosenthal, David. 'Rated 'H' for Horrors.' *New York* (February 18, 1980): 50–4.

Rothman, William. *The 'I' of the Camera: Essays in Film Criticism, History, and Aesthetics.* Second Edition. Cambridge: Cambridge University Press, 2004.

Ryan, Michael and Douglas Kellner. *Camera Politica: The Politics and Ideology of Contemporary Hollywood Film.* Bloomington: Indiana University Press, 1988, 114-28.

Schechter, Harold. *The Bosom Serpent: Folklore and Popular Art.* Iowa City: University of Iowa Press, 1988.

Sconce, Jeffrey. *Haunted Media: Electronic Presence from Telegraphy to Television.* Durham, NC: Duke University Press, 2000.

Sexton, Jamie. 'US 'Indie-Horror': Critical Reception, Genre Construction, and Suspect Hybridity.' *Cinema Journal* 51.2 (2012): 67–86.

Short, Sue. *Misfit Sisters: Screen Horror as Female Rites of Passage.* Houndmills: Palgrave Macmillan, 2006.

Singer, Ben. *Melodrama and Modernity: Early Sensational Cinema and its Contexts.* New York: Columbia University Press, 2001.

Skal, David J. *Death Makes a Holiday: A Cultural History of Halloween*. New York: Bloomsbury, 2002.

Skal, David J. *The Monster Show: A Cultural History of Horror*. Revised Edition. New York: Faber and Faber, 2001.

Smith, Don. G. *H.P. Lovecraft in Popular Culture: The Works and Their Adaptations in Film, Television, Comics, Music and Games*. Jefferson: McFarland, 2006.

Spadoni, Robert. *Uncanny Bodies: The Coming of Sound Film and the Origins of the Horror Genre*. Berkeley: University of California Press, 2007.

Stableford, Richard. 'The Cosmic Horror.' *Icons of Horror and the Supernatural: An Encyclopedia of Our Worst Nightmares*. V.1. Westport: Greenwood Press, 2007, 65-96.

Stone, Gregory P. 'Halloween and the Mass Child.' *American Quarterly* 11.3 (Autumn 1959): 372–79.

Telotte, J.P. 'Through a Pumpkin's Eye: The Reflexive Nature of Horror.' *American Horrors: Essays on the Modern American Horror Film*. Ed. Gregory A. Waller. Chicago: University of Illinois Press, 1987.

Thurschwell, Pamela. *Literature, Technology and Magical Thinking, 1880-1920*. Cambridge: Cambridge University Press, 2001.

Todorov, Tzvetan. *The Fantastic: A Structural Approach to a Literary Genre*. Cleveland: Press of Case Western Reserve University, 1973.

Trencansky, Sarah. 'Final Girls and Terrible Youth: Transgression in 1980s Slasher Horror.' *Journal of Popular Film & Television* 29.2 (2001): 63–73.

Williams, Linda. 'Film Madness: The Uncanny Return of the Repressed in Polanski's *The Tenant*.' *Cinema Journal* 20.2 (Spring 1981): 63–73.

Williams, Tony. *Hearths of Darkness: The Family in the American Horror Film*. Madison: Fairleigh Dickinson University Press, 1996.

Wood, Robin. 'An Introduction to the American Horror Film.' *The American Nightmare*. Toronto: Festival of Festivals, 1979a, 7-28.

Wood, Robin. *Hollywood from Vietnam to Reagan*. New York: Columbia University Press, 1986.

Wood, Robin. *Personal Views: Explorations in Film*. Revised Edition. Detroit: Wayne State University Press, 2006.

Wood, Robin. 'Sisters.' *The American Nightmare*. Toronto: Festival of Festivals, 1979b, 59-64.

Yablans, Irwin. *The Man Who Created Halloween*. North Charleston, SC: CreateSpace, 2012.

Zinoman, Jason. *Shock Value: How a Few Eccentric Outsiders Gave Us Nightmares, Conquered Hollywood and Invented Modern Horror*. New York: Penguin Press, 2011.

Zimbardo, Philip G. 'A Situationist Perspective on the Psychology of Evil: Understanding How Good People Are Transformed into Perpetrators.' *The Social Psychology of Good and Evil*. Ed. Arthur G. Miller. New York: The Guildford Press, 2004, 21-50.

Žižek, Slavoj. *Looking Awry: An Introduction to Jacques Lacan through Popular Culture*. Cambridge: MIT, 1991.

DEVIL'S ADVOCATES

"Auteur Publishing's new Devil's Advocates critiques on individual titles offer bracingly fresh perspectives from passionate writers. The series will perfectly complement the BFI archive volumes." Christopher Fowler, Independent on Sunday

LET THE RIGHT ONE IN — ANNE BILLSON

"Anne Billson offers an accessible, lively but thoughtful take on the '80s-set Swedish vampire belter... a fun, stimulating exploration of a modern masterpiece." Empire

WITCHFINDER GENERAL — IAN COOPER

"I enjoyed it very much; it sets out all the various influences, both before and after the film, and indeed the essence of the film itself, very well indeed." Jonathan Rigby, author of English Gothic

SAW — BENJAMIN POOLE

"This is a great addition to a series of books that are starting to become compulsory for horror fans. It will also help you to appreciate just what an original and amazing experience the original SAW truly was." The Dark Side

THE TEXAS CHAIN SAW MASSACRE — JAMES ROSE

"[James Rose] find[s] new and unusual perspectives with which to address [the] censor-baiting material. Unsurprisingly, the effect... is to send the reader back to the films... watch the films, read these Devil's Advocate analyses of them." Crime Time

Printed and bound by CPI Group (UK) Ltd, Croydon, CR0 4YY

13/04/2025

14656608-0001